Also by Peter R. Breggin, M.D.

Medication Madness: The Role of Psychiatric Drugs in Cases of Violence, Suicide, and Crime (2008)

Brain-Disabling Treatments in Psychiatry: Drugs, Electroshock and the Psychopharmaceutical Complex, Second Edition (2008)

Toxic Psychiatry: Why Therapy, Empathy and Love Must Replace the Drugs, Electroshock and Biochemical Theories of the "New Psychiatry" (1991)

Your Drug May Be Your Problem: How and Why To Stop Taking Psychiatric Medications, Second Edition (coauthor David Cohen) (2007)

Beyond Conflict: From Self-Help and Psychotherapy to Peacemaking (1992)

Talking Back to Prozac (coauthor Ginger Breggin) (1994)

Psychosocial Approaches to Deeply Disturbed Persons (coeditor E. Mark Stern) (1996)

The Heart of Being Helpful: Empathy and the Creation of a Healing Presence (1997)

The War Against Children of Color: Psychiatry Targets Inner City Children (coauthor Ginger Breggin) (1998)

Reclaiming Our Children: A Healing Solution for a Nation in Crisis (2000)

Talking Back to Ritalin, Revised Edition (2001)

The Antidepressant Fact Book (2001)

Dimensions of Empathic Therapy (coeditors Ginger Breggin and Fred Bemak) (2002)

The Ritalin Fact Book (2002)

About Dr. Breggin

The Conscience of Psychiatry: The Reform Work of Peter R. Breggin, MD (edited by the International Center for the Study of Psychiatry and Psychology) (2009)

Wow, I'm an American!

Wow, I'm an American!

How to Live Like Our Nation's Heroic Founders

A Book for the Whole Family

by Peter R. Breggin, MD

Lake Edge Press
Ithaca, New York

Wow, I'm An American!
How to Live Like Our Nation's Heroic Founders
A Lake Edge Press Book

Printing History
Lake Edge Press / 2009

Cover photograph and book design
by Ginger Ross Breggin

For information address:
Lake Edge Press
101 East State Street, No. 112, Ithaca, New York 14850

ISBN: 978-0-9824560-1-9

1. United States-History-Revolution
2. Social Values-United States 3. Psychology 4. Inspirational

My wife Ginger and I were married
On the Fourth of July
Twenty-five years ago
Amid fireworks.

This book is dedicated to Ginger
And to our friend, Brian Kean
Who helped me accept
The Invisible Hand in my life.

The Primary Principles

Protect freedom.
Take responsibility at all times.
Express gratitude for every gift and opportunity.
Become a source of love.

TABLE OF CONTENTS

Introduction	Live Like an American!	1
Chapter 1	Alive in America	5
Chapter 2	John Adams: On the King's "Most Wanted" List	21
Chapter 3	Our Declaration to the World About Freedom	35
Chapter 4	Who Made Up These Ideas About Liberty?	51
Chapter 5	Freedom: Growing Like Butterfly Bushes in America	67
Chapter 6	George Washington: The Greatest Man Alive	81
Chapter 7	Benjamin Franklin: The Most Generous Founder	101
Chapter 8	The U. S. Constitution—Our Ship of Freedom	117
Chapter 9	The Bill of Rights—Our Shield of Freedom	129
Chapter 10	Keeping the Wow! in America	143
Chapter 11	When "Dependence" Meets "Independence"	151
Chapter 12	Become a Source of Love	167
Chapter 13	A Friend Who Lived By Basic American Values	191
Chapter 14	The Four Primary Principles of a Good Life	199
Chapter 15	Applying The Primary Principles to Our Lives	205
	Bibliography	223
	Notes	227
	Acknowledgements	232
	About the Author	234

Key Dates

1765 The Stamp Act

1770 The Boston Massacre

1773 The Boston Tea Party

1774 The First Continental Congress

1775 The Second Continental Congress

Fighting at Lexington and Concord

George Washington chosen Commander-in-Chief of the Army

The Battle of Bunker Hill

1776 Thomas Paine writes Common Sense

The Declaration of Independence

Washington crosses the Delaware

1777 The Continental Army winters at Valley Forge

1781 The British surrender at Yorktown

1783 The Treaty of Paris ends the war

1787 The Constitutional Convention

1788 The Constitution of the United States

1789 George Washington elected first President of the United States

1791 The Bill of Rights

1796 George Washington's Farewell Address

1796 John Adams elected second President of the United States

1800 Thomas Jefferson elected third President of the United States

Introduction

Live Like an American!

What the Founders accomplished lives on today, not only in our government and its great documents—but also in the principles and values embedded in our hearts as Americans. This book is about those values and how they can guide us through the good times and the bad times both as a nation and as individuals in our everyday lives.

The Founders not only gave the world a model government, they provided us personal examples for how to live ethical, satisfying, and happy lives. The Founders hoped that their new American government and its ideals would increase the opportunity for human happiness. They have been proven right not only in the government they created, but also in the principles they have given us to guide our personal lives.

One Set of Values for Every Purpose

The Founders of our nation—men and women like George and Martha Washington, and John and Abigail Adams—tried to live every day by the same ideals that caused them to commit their lives to the War of Independence. The war was fought not only by men, but also by women and even children who managed the family homes, farms, and businesses while the men were away. These women and children often endured as much suffering and displayed as much determination as the men, and they too provide us inspiration on how to live our own lives.

None Betrayed Their Principles

We will find that not a single signer of the Declaration of Independence, and not a single wife of a signer, ever withdrew support from what they called the great Cause. Under the most dangerous and disastrous personal circumstances, they lived by their principles. We are indebted to the Founding Families for creating this nation and for setting so many consistent examples of how to live life courageously, ethically, and successfully. We can live by these same ideals; we owe it to them, to ourselves, and to future generations.

For the Founders, their love for political liberty dovetailed with their devotion to personal freedom and responsibility. Political liberty could not survive without citizens exercising personal responsibility for themselves and their families, their communities, the nation, and even humankind. John Adams explained, "Liberty can no more exist without virtue and independence, than the body can live and move without a soul."[1]

The Founders did not put God in one pocket, politics in another, and their personal conduct in yet another. For them, understanding all of life began with understanding human nature. What God wanted of human beings was expressed in human nature. Human nature therefore provided the key to how we should act in every aspect of our lives including government, religion, and the details of our daily choices.

The Founders not only built the foundation for the most marvelous nation in history—they provided us the guidelines for living a good life. This integrity—this consistency and wholeness of values in every aspect of life—is one of their greatest and least recognized gifts to us. In the words of Abigail Adams, "and if we have not wealth, we have what is better, Integrity."[2]

It took courage for Abigail to live by these principles and it takes courage for each of us to live by them as well. Living a principled life requires hard work and courage—but it is the only way to live a good and satisfying life.

The Primary Principles

To their extraordinary credit, the Founders looked into their own human nature and into God's vision of how human beings should relate to each other, and came up with a plan for government and an approach to everyday life that promoted enduring core ideals. These values are captured in what I call The Primary Principles:

The Primary Principles
Protect freedom.
Take responsibility at all times.
Express gratitude for all your gifts and opportunities.
Become a source of love.

As this book examines momentous events such as the signing of the Declaration of Independence, the winning of the War of Independence, and the creation of the Constitution and Bill of Rights—never forget that the individual Founders brought to these tasks their personal ethical standards and understanding of life. We can use their principles and their wisdom to direct and improve our own lives and those of our families.

Human values are seamless; they are sewn into every inch of the fabric of our lives from the personal to the political. America's founding principles can inspire us with courage and help us to reclaim our personal lives while we work toward reclaiming our government.

Have Hope

We should not despair at the increasing loss of Founding values in the political arena. To begin with, we can implement these enduring values in our personal lives regardless of what happens in the public arena. We can guarantee ourselves to make every effort to live by the principles of freedom, responsibility, gratitude, and love, even while our politicians fail us time and again. We can be brave while the politicians run for cover. We can remain determined to do what's right despite their habitual compromising. In short, we can do a great deal more to control and to improve ourselves as individuals than we can do to change the direction or to impede the momentum of our glacial government.

Many wise persons have observed that change begins within ourselves, and that through our own ethical growth we can give more to everyone we touch. In improving ourselves, we enhance the lives of everyone around us. And as we grow in numbers, we can ultimately revive America by returning our great nation to its Founding roots in freedom, responsibility, gratitude, and love. I offer you *Wow, I'm an American!* to renew your vision of what makes America great, to further inspire you to make your own life more satisfying and even heroic, and to share these values with your loved ones and family.

Chapter One

Alive in America

Most of us are incredibly fortunate. When we wake up in the morning, we are alive in America. It's worth savoring this miracle—Alive in the United States of America! We can look around and say, "Wow, I'm an American! I'm free. I can try to become anything I want. I can develop my abilities and pursue my desires."

If it seems naïve or even shallow to express such unbridled enthusiasm about being an American, think of the millions of refugees from around the world who have left everything behind and risked their lives for this opportunity. From Vietnamese who escaped to freedom in leaky, overcrowded boats to Cubans and Haitians who set out for our coast clinging to makeshift rafts, their death-defying efforts to get here demonstrate their desire to become Americans. You can see the same enthusiasm in the happy faces of immigrants when they take the oath to become American citizens. Most people come to America eagerly seeking freedom and the opportunity to take responsibility for themselves and their families.

If it still seems unsophisticated to voice such gratitude and enthusiasm for being an American, imagine being unceremoniously ripped out of your current surroundings and deposited in almost any other nation in the world. England, Canada, or Australia might not bring on much culture shock—because, frankly, they have benefited from America's values and from her heroic efforts to defend their freedom against violent oppressors like Nazi Germany, Imperial Japan, and the USSR. But instead of finding yourself in a relatively free Western nation, imagine if you landed instead in Russia, China, Cuba, North Korea, Iran, Sudan, or any number of nations that reject the liberating influence of our Founders and their War of Independence. Putting aside the language barrier, think about the values barrier.

Better yet, imagine being thrust back in time before there was a United States of America—before the Declaration of Independence and the Bill of Rights transformed the world. Until the colonists fought for and won their independence, in the entire world there was nothing like the country that we now live in—not a single other place where you could say, "I can take responsibility for myself and make the most of my life."

Planning the Best Possible Nation in the World

The United States of America didn't just happen. Freedom never "just happens." More than two hundred years ago, people fought for the freedom that you and I now enjoy. And during the struggle for liberty, they began making plans for a nation that they wanted to remain free for all of us to enjoy in the future.

A Letter by George Washington (1783)[3]

The foundation of our Empire was not laid in the gloomy age of Ignorance and Superstition, but at an Epoch when the rights of mankind were better understood and more clearly defined, than at any former period... At this auspicious period, the United States came into existence as a Nation, and if their Citizens should not be completely free and happy, the fault will be entirely their own.

This new approach to government began with the idea of human rights—freedom from the kinds of oppressive traditions, authoritarian religious institutions, and totalitarian governments that dominated life in Europe at the time. The Founders of the nation believed that the proper role of government is the protection of human rights. Political liberty would provide the opportunity for people to work responsibly toward achieving personal happiness. They were very explicit about the right to seek individual happiness.

Nowadays people too often want the government to take care of their needs and to help other people who cannot help themselves. Politicians talk about providing safety and security. They almost never speak of providing freedom for people to pursue their own happiness. Can you recall hearing a politician speak about government providing people the opportunity to become "happier" on their own? The Founders frequently spoke in those glowing, joyful terms. They wanted people to be free to find their own happiness. The responsibility was theirs.

Never forget that the Founders saw the government's primary purpose as providing opportunity—to protect the freedom of individuals to achieve happiness through their own hard work and ability. The government defends liberty; the rest is up to you and me. And the American Revolution was only the beginning. The Founders wanted this same opportunity for liberty and happiness for all humankind. They often spoke about their devotion to the future of humanity around the world.

Historian John Ferling about John Adams[4]

For Adams, the American Revolution was about opportunity: the opportunity for people to govern themselves and for the individual to achieve whatever his merit could earn. If humankind could thus be liberated to pursue happiness, Adams believed, people at last would have before them the opportunity to achieve the "greatest Quantity of Happiness."

America's Founders knew that human beings and human nature were imperfect. We all have flaws. But they saw within human nature a glorious potential instilled by nature and by God—a potential for responsibility, productivity, and happiness that was only possible in a nation as free as America could become. In *Washington's God* (2006), Michael Novak and Jana Novak describe George Washington's credo: "Washington located the universal fuel supply of the sacred fire of liberty in human nature itself."[5]

Many Separate Flags

I want you to imagine this along with me because it's quite amazing. We are looking at the world more than two hundred years ago and there is no Constitution of the United States of America. The War of Independence has been won; but the nation is barely more than a collection of independent states that govern themselves and jealously guard their own independence. It's 1787 and several dozen men we now call the Founders—the leaders who created this nation—have come together from all across the colonies to meet in Philadelphia. Originally they planned to revise the existing Articles of Confederation that provided for a loose coalition of autonomous states. But in a dramatic assertion of their wills they determined to tear up the old document and to start from scratch to build the first government in history based on reason and sound principles.

For days on end, they talked and argued about the laws that would govern the new nation—the new Constitution of the United States of America. Sometimes they took breaks to go back home to share their latest ideas. They hiked, rode horses or horse-drawn carriages hundreds of miles to talk over their new ideas with neighbors and friends. Then they returned to Philadelphia to continue their heated discussions about how to build the best possible government for themselves and future generations, including you and me.

The Founders were very aware that their decisions and actions would influence posterity, including folks like you and me. We should never forget this—people fought and people worked hard to create the country that we now enjoy. They put an enormous amount of thought into it and were acutely aware of acting on behalf of humankind and posterity.

But I'm getting ahead of the story. Before the Founders could begin to plan a government for the United States, they had to fight for their independence from King George III of England whose British Empire spread across the globe. Later it would be said that the sun never set on the British Empire.

Before there was a United States of America, there were of course thirteen separate colonies that ran from north to south down the east coast of the American continent. Each had its own government with its own laws and even its own flag. Virginia had one set of laws and a unique flag, and so did New Hampshire, Massachusetts, Connecticut, New York, New Jersey, Pennsylvania, Rhode Island, Delaware, Maryland, North and South Carolina, and Georgia. People in each of the separate colonies already enjoyed a great deal of freedom. They felt independent—able to make their own decisions and choices in many aspects of their lives.

The colonists enjoyed a measure of freedom but they did not have the final say about everything that was important to them. Each of the colonies was under the control of Great Britain—a government so far away that it took many weeks to travel there, or to send and receive communications, by the fastest sailing ships.

Some colonists were fond of making fun of the King as a pretentious little man who lived on a tiny island off the coast of Europe that was too far away from America to matter. But with his armies and his great navy, he ruled a large part of the world.

In those days, no one said, "I pledge allegiance to the flag of the United States of America." There was no American flag and it would be treasonous to pledge allegiance to any except the British flag, called the Union Jack. It was treasonous to disobey and to defy the king's law; it was punishable by death.

A Bunch of Unruly Children

The first British colony in America was established in 1607 in Jamestown, Virginia, and twelve years later for the first time in America representatives met together in Jamestown as a legislative body. Then in 1620 the Mayflower landed with the Pilgrims on the coast of Massachusetts and the new colonists signed the Mayflower Compact in which they agreed to make decisions by majority rule and to dedicate themselves to the general welfare.

These events set in motion the development of the British colonies in America with Virginia and Massachusetts taking the lead in size and in economic and political importance. By 1700 there were 250,000 English people colonizing America and by 1776, when American declared its independence, it had grown rapidly to 2 million. From the start, there was a streak of independence in these colonists and a desire to rule themselves.

In 1760 a young King George III took the throne of England. Initially he continued the practice of allowing the colonies to make many of their own laws and regulations. But he wanted them to acknowledge who was ultimately in charge. According to King George, he was totally in charge. Why? Because he said so, and millions of people around the world believed that he was right. For thousands of years, people had grown used to being told what to do by kings and other tyrannical rulers. The more powerful classes in these societies—warriors, priests, scholars, and owners of property and wealth—generally supported these rulers to their own advantage. Meanwhile the vast majority of people were kept in their place in grinding poverty century after century.

In those days, ordinary people didn't think about "progress" or making the world a better place. They didn't think about making plans to greatly improve their own lives or their children's lives. They thought about surviving and getting by, staying out of trouble, and taking care of their families as best they could.

Even before they rebelled against the king, the American colonists already enjoyed much more freedom than any other people in the world. That was in part because they lived so far away from the king that he could not control their everyday activities. But having so much freedom only made the Americans want more. They yearned to become more independent, but they were not eager to get into a fight with the British king. The Americans and the British were in many ways like a family. They spoke the same language and many shared the same religion. Many Americans loved and respected the king and thought of England as the Mother Country. They had come from England and still had brothers and sisters, parents and grandparents living on the island across the Atlantic.

Thomas Hutchinson was a public official in Massachusetts and was among the king's most loyal subjects and advocates in America. In a show of sympathy for his king, he quoted a biblical verse, "I have nourished children and brought them up, and even they have revolted from me." As his fellow colonists continued to rebel, Hutchinson hung onto the hope that Great Britain would exercise its authority over the American colonies "in the same gentle, tender manner that a parent exercises his authority over his children."

The "parent" of a big family, yes, but King George increasingly viewed the Americans as a bunch of unruly, ungrateful children who needed to be disciplined.

Hutchinson failed to appreciate that "Americans were no longer children and would not pretend to be. The metaphor had been outgrown. Thousands of citizens in the colonies had been swept into the struggle and had become Sons of Liberty rather than sons of a living king across the sea."[6]

King George was not destined to remain the father of our family. Our Founding Mothers and Fathers became our real parents, and they would establish a nation aimed at guaranteeing our freedoms from tyrants like King George.

Taxation Without Representation

The American colonists were especially outraged that King George wanted to impose taxes on them. Any government needs money to support itself, including paying for government workers and officials, and supporting its army and navy. It gains most of its money by taxation—seizing a portion of the wealth that its people own or produce.

Collecting taxes is the government's most important power. Hopefully, the government uses the money wisely for the benefit of the people by maintaining police agencies, armed forces, a court system, transportation, education, support for the poor, and other useful services. Hopefully, it doesn't take away too much money from the people by taxing them too harshly. Regardless of the government, these hopes for restraint in taxing and spending usually remain unfulfilled.

Even King George was limited in how much he could tax his subjects. At the time, England already had a Parliament with a House of Commons that was made of representatives who were elected to balance the king's power. Parliament could pass laws, including how much to tax everyone in the British Empire.

The Americans resented being taxed by King George and Parliament. The colonists were not allowed to elect their own representatives to Parliament and complained with a famous slogan, "No taxation without representation." They also argued that England was too far away to demand taxes from them or to provide useful services in return.

At first the great majority of the Founders and most other colonists did not want to make war against the king. Instead, they hoped he would leave them alone to enjoy the freedom they already possessed. If King George had agreed to limit or to stop taxing the Americans, they might not have gone to war. But the king wouldn't leave them alone. Instead, he got madder and meaner, and the colonists reacted by becoming more rebellious.

In a particularly insulting action, the king imposed the infamous Stamp Act on the American colonies in1765. The Stamp Act required an official government stamp on almost all printed matter including legal documents, newspapers, pamphlets and even playing cards. Only books and private letters were exempted.

In protest, a leader of the Boston insurrection named Samuel Adams authored a series of resolutions in the Massachusetts legislature that affirmed God as a higher authority than the king: "Resolved, that there are certain essential rights ... which are founded in the law of God and nature, and are the common rights of all mankind." This world-shaking concept of universal rights emanating from God and nature would echo through the next decade until finding its full expression in the Declaration of Independence. Another resolution of Samuel Adams emphasized property: "Resolved, that no man can justly take the property of another without his consent." Adams's biographer observed, "These two prongs of the American argument—God and property rights—would be used by Adams and the colonists all the way from 1765 through independence and beyond."[7] Samuel's cousin John Adams eloquently confirmed this exact viewpoint when he wrote, "the moment the idea is admitted into society that property is not as sacred as the laws of God, and there is not a force of law and public justice to protect it, anarchy and tyranny commence."[8]

The colonists were so outraged that the king reluctantly revoked the Stamp Act, but not before reasserting his basic right to tax and to control the colonies. More taxes and greater restrictions on freedom would follow in the next ten years leading up to the War of Independence.

Meanwhile, even Sam Adams was not yet ready to openly challenge the king's authority to govern. Until the bitter end most of the Founders kept asking for a compromise; but the monarch felt too threatened by their rebelliousness and by their ideas about freedom.

King George was right to feel threatened. Once it got rolling, the idea of freedom would gather overwhelming momentum. It began in America but soon kings all over the world would discover to their dismay that people no longer felt compelled to believed in or to obey them.

A Snake Cut into Pieces

The Americans weren't spoiling for a fight and they were not that enthusiastic about building a big national government of their own. Each of the thirteen colonies valued its own ways and separateness, and each thought of itself almost like an independent country. But joining together became the only way to resist the king's taxes and defend themselves from his armed forces. A famous cartoon, published at the time by Benjamin Franklin, showed a snake cut into pieces representing the different regions and colonies. Only by joining together could the colonies fight and win.

Hardships in Gathering Together

When the Founders gathered in Philadelphia in 1774 at the First Continental Congress to discuss among themselves their conflicts with King George and to debate possible independence from Great Britain, they traveled many days and sometimes weeks along rocky, muddy, snowy, or icy roads. Riding in carriages with no springs was a dangerous ordeal. In winter the roads were sheets of broken ice. In summer, they became mud holes. Every time a carriage wheel hit a rock or rut, the force was driven upward into the spines of the passengers.

Living in Philadelphia wasn't easy either. Epidemics were so deadly that the Founders at times fled the city to keep from catching fatal infectious diseases like yellow fever, small pox, and malaria.

In addition, the Founders left behind their families, their businesses, and their farms or plantations. Great burdens were placed on their wives and older children who had to take over. In coming chapters, we shall learn more about what the Founding Families went through.

The Shot Heard 'Round the World

In April 1775 while the American leaders were gathering in Philadelphia, the British marched from Boston into the countryside to impose the royal will on the rebellious colonists and to seize a storehouse full of weapons at Concord. They also wanted to capture two of the more notorious "rebels," Samuel Adams and John Hancock who were meeting in the countryside. When they heard that the British were coming, Adams and Hancock wanted to fight alongside the militiamen; but their colleagues refused to put their leaders at risk.[9]

Messengers on horseback, including Paul Revere on his famous ride, alerted the colonists. Church bells sounded the alarm, bringing armed colonists streaming in from the surrounding countryside to resist the British incursion. Shots were fired, perhaps initially by accident, and then fighting broke out. The British began to retreat toward Lexington on their way back to Boston. The sound of gunfire echoed over the countryside, drawing more colonists into the fight.

The colonists took advantage of the terrain. Shooting at the king's soldiers from behind trees, boulders and rock walls, and out of the windows of homes, the Americans rained destruction on the retreating column. Called Redcoats because of the color of their impressive uniforms, these highly trained and disciplined soldiers were primed to rush with fixed bayonets at the enemy, but they could find no one to charge. Instead, their red coats made fine targets. In frustration and panic, the harassed soldiers retreated in disorder.

Of 900 British soldiers who marched into the countryside, more than 270 were wounded or killed, while the Americans suffered fewer than 100 casualties.[10]

The Meaning of Casualties

Words like "casualties" are easily passed over. Even "wounded and killed" won't strike home to us unless we pause to think imaginatively and empathically about it. Although it happened more than two hundred years ago, we should remember that the soldiers who died—Redcoats and Americans alike—were actual living people. Innocent civilians caught in the conflict were actual living people.

It is easy to think that the British soldiers were "bad" and that the Americans were "good." All this would become less clear to us if we knew the individuals personally. On both sides, we would find some people admirable and we would find some wanting. The difference would lie mainly in the governments and the principles that they were fighting for.

In wars, real people are killed and injured, lives are ruined; and many wars are wholly unjustified, accomplish nothing good, or make things worse. But freedom cannot survive without people risking their lives by fighting for it. Freedom and democracy cannot survive without being defended and without people at times sacrificing their lives.

From the Diary of a British Officer at Lexington and Concord[11]

As the Country for many miles around Boston and in the neighborhood of Lexington and Concord had by this time had notice of what was doing, as well as by the firing, as from the expresses which had been [sent] from Boston and the adjacent places in all directions, numbers of armed men on foot and horseback were continually coming from all parts guided by the fire, and before the Column had advanced a mile on the road, we were fired at from all quarters, but particularly from the houses on the roadside and the Adjacent Stone Walls. Several of the Troops were killed and wounded in this way, and the soldiers were so enraged at the suffering from an unseen Enemy that they forced open many of the houses from which the fire proceeded and put to death all those found in them...

A little more than one hundred years after its last armed conflict with Great Britain in the War of 1812, America entered World War I in 1916 and then World War II in 1941. Now independent of Great Britain, we did this in part to help preserve the freedom and democracy of this same British people. Massive wars with thousands and even millions of causalities—it's not the world we would wish for, but it's the world that has been given to us, one in which we must at times fight to preserve our freedom and the freedom of other nations.

Before the Revolutionary War was over, an estimated 25,000 Americans would die for the freedom and democracy that we have today. Another 25,000 would be wounded. Tens of thousands would have their lives disrupted or ruined. Modern America is a monument to these casualties and to the casualties of all our wars for freedom. These martyrs not only set the stage for our government, they provided us principles to live by in our everyday lives.

The gunfire that started the battle of Lexington and Concord was later called "The shot heard round world."[12] It signaled the start of open warfare between the colonists and the British, leading eventually to American independence and the spread of the idea of freedom.

The Americans won that first skirmish against the British; but the British army was the mightiest in the world and it might suddenly appear at any time searching for the Founders in Philadelphia or wherever they might be hiding.

Where's the American Army?

There was no way of communicating over long distances—no telephone lines or cell phones. No radios or TVs. The Founders—meeting in Philadelphia at the Second Continental Congress—were in danger of being awakened almost any morning by the cry, "The British are coming!" The king's soldiers could sail up the river, land nearby, and march on Philadelphia before America's leaders could escape. By the time Founders like John Adams and George Washington got out of their beds, the dreaded soldiers might have cut off their escape. More than once, the Founders would have to escape Philadelphia with the British in hot pursuit.

What about the American army? Couldn't our army defend the Founders when they were meeting in Philadelphia?

In the beginning there was no American army. Each of the colonies had its own local military organization called a militia. The militia was not a professional army. It was made up mostly of civilians who volunteered to take up arms when necessary to defend their colony. A man would hear the church bells ring, grab his gun, and run to the village square to gather with other men in defense of their homes.

In Virginia, for example, the militia fought the Indians and sometimes they fought alongside the British against the French who still claimed part of North America. But there was no American army to fight the King of Great Britain. Like everything else about the new nation, the army had to be planned and made to happen. Two men would play key roles, John Adams in planning the army and George Washington in leading it.

You can see how confusing everything was in the beginning. The colonists resented being taxed by King George and his Parliament and they harbored deep convictions about the inviolability of their property and their freedom. The Founders were meeting in Philadelphia, but some were not ready to declare complete independence from Great Britain. Meanwhile, local groups of colonists were already battling with guns against the king's army in Massachusetts; but the war remained undeclared. And nobody knew where the British might turn up next—maybe in New York, maybe in Philadelphia, maybe deep in the southern colonies.

But beneath the confusion something was going on that would change the world. New ideas were brewing—ideas about independence from the British Empire, about freedom and, most important of all, about human rights—about life, liberty, property, and the pursuit of happiness. These ideas were being debated at the Congress and talked about throughout the colonies.

Human rights means that that every single person in the world has basic rights such as freedom, the right to own property, and the right to pursue his or her own life and happiness. This put limits or restraints on democracy. Even when people have the right to vote, they must not take away the right of individuals to pursue their own lives. Until this moment in colonial America, in the great expanse of time there had never been a nation anywhere that recognized and protected the individual human rights of its citizens.

Resentment against King George was growing into something much greater—the Cause that would create a nation that would become a beacon of freedom and human rights to the whole world.

Chapter Two

John Adams: On the King's "Most Wanted" List

Our country has recently been going through an extraordinary financial and economic crisis in part because too many people in positions of responsibility failed to stand up for what's right. Some in Congress pandered to their constituents by pushing for housing programs for the poor that were bound to fail when the recipients could not keep up with their mortgage payments. Some in business made fortunes from selling these shaky mortgages in large combined batches that were impossible to evaluate. Others who knew what was going on didn't dare to tell the truth that the country was heading for financial disaster. The U. S. Congress and one president after another went full steam ahead while the housing market overheated and corporate speculators made outlandish profits.

No one seemed to remember the Founding principles of the nation and especially the observation repeated by Washington, John Adams and other Founders that freedom would forever depend upon an ethical and responsible citizenry. The abandonment of principle had its dreadful and inevitable result. The free market became a free for all, and then went into free fall. Moral bankruptcy became financial bankruptcy.

John Adams represents a stark contrast to this moral chaos. Among the most influential and hardworking Founders, he was willing to do what he knew was right, even when doing what's right made other people displeased with him and even when it endangered his income and career. He believed that our new nation had to make room for people to say and do what they believed was right, even if the majority didn't agree. He wanted people to have individual rights and he wouldn't compromise about it.

John was not perfect and he made personal and political mistakes. The reader can find innumerable books that flesh out his every fault. But far more importantly, he helped in extraordinary ways to make this country into a place where you can wake up with the hope of making a good life for yourself and your loved ones. His underlying principles and values, and his heroic, hardworking efforts, provide us a model for how to "Live like an American!"

A Dangerous Reputation

As America moved toward declaring its independence from the British, the British knew many of the rebellious Founders by name and reputation, including John Adams. Adams was a man of principle. He had ideas about right and wrong, including fairness and honesty, and he tried to put these principles ahead of everything else. He insisted on being fair and honest even when it got him into trouble and made his friends angry with him. Eventually he would become a marked man—at the very top of the king's "most wanted" list of American "criminals."

Standing Up for "The Bad Guys"

When Americans began to demand more independence from the British Empire, King George sent a garrison to intimidate the people of Boston. The king didn't think he needed to send a large army that would drain his royal treasury. He thought that most of the people of Boston were loyal to him—that they believed in him and wanted to obey him. And he thought his enemies were weaklings and cowards. But the people in Boston were getting very irritated and frustrated with the king and his attempts to exert more power over them.

One cold winter day an angry group of Americans started threatening a group of British soldiers, backing them up against a wall. Then the group turned into a mob, hurling chunks of ice and other objects at the soldiers. The streets were paved with heavy bricks called cobblestones and some people in the crowd may have picked up loose cobblestones to hurl at the soldiers.

The British soldiers became terrified and without receiving an order from their commander, they fired their long rifles into the crowd, killing five people. This enraged the citizens of Boston. The Redcoats were jailed and made to stand trial for murder. Angry Bostonians called the shooting a massacre. Posters showing the "Boston massacre" were nailed to trees and buildings for everyone to see. The year was 1770—six years before America would declare its independence.

John Adams was a successful young lawyer in Boston when the British soldiers implored John to defend them. Can you imagine that—defending enemy soldiers when everyone you know hates them for shooting and killing your friends and neighbors?

John's friends warned him, "John, you cannot defend the Redcoats. Everyone in Boston hates them. People will hate you for defending them. Your career will be over."

John Adams wanted people to like him. Anecdotes about him indicate that he was very sensitive to what people thought of him. His feelings were easily hurt. He was also ambitious and eager for public acclaim. But he believed in fairness even more than he wanted to be liked, even more than he wanted to make money or to become rich and famous.

John carefully examined what had happened during the Boston massacre. He interviewed witnesses and he met with the soldiers, some of whom were mere boys. He felt sympathy and understanding for them. He realized that the seemingly formidable Redcoats had actually been confused and frightened for their lives when they fired their guns into the angry mob that was pressing in on them.

After talking it over with his wife Abigail, John made up his mind to defend the Redcoats in court in front of a jury made up of men from Boston. John knew that the men on the jury resented the king and his soldiers, and wanted to get even with them. John was left with the difficult task of convincing the jurors to be fair to the soldiers.

It looked as if John Adams would lose the trial and that the soldiers would be hanged. But John asked his fellow Bostonians in the jury to put aside their prejudice against the king's men. He asked them to be fair to them as individual human beings. This idea of protecting the rights of individuals would become a foundation stone for the building of our nation.

John successfully convinced the jury to be fair. The captain of the soldiers was exonerated and only two of the soldiers were punished. No one was hanged.

You might think that King George would be very impressed with John Adams. After all, John had defended the king's soldiers and saved them from death. But the king was more interested in power than in justice. How dare the Americans put his troops on trial!

After America declared its independence in 1776, King George especially feared and resented John Adams. So the king instructed his soldiers to capture John and to hang him by the neck until dead. It's worth taking a moment to imagine how John Adams must have felt, living under the threat of a cruel death. That's how much he and the other Founders believed in building a country where citizens could be free to live their own lives as they chose. To this very day, their bravery gives us the opportunity to enjoy our freedom. Their bravery can also inspire in us the courage to live principled lives of our own.

Although they were not perfect, many of the Founders tried to conduct their lives by the same principles that led them to fight for freedom and independence. They wanted to respect each other's rights and to live independent and responsible lives. John Adams remains a marvelous example to us.

The King Gets Tougher and Tensions Grow

King George and the British Parliament continued to tighten their control over the colonies. For example, Great Britain limited the rights of American ships to trade freely with the remainder of the world. American ship owners responded by smuggling; they carried forbidden goods on their ships. John Hancock—the first signer of the Declaration of Independence, whose signature is famous for being by far the most prominent—owned a ship named Liberty. The British captured his ship and Hancock was charged with smuggling. John Adams successfully defended him in court.

The conflict heightened when the British passed laws that put a heavy tax on tea, and also made it impossible for Americans to sell or even to smuggle their tea at a profit. In the Boston Tea Party in December 1773, colonists raided ships full of tea in Boston harbor. In an act of defiance against Great Britain, they dressed as Indians and threw overboard 90,000 pounds of tea with an estimated worth of several million dollars. To Americans this is a famous event; to the British at the time, it was infamous. It showed the Americans to be a lawless mob.

Colonial leaders were already beginning to see the looming struggle for independence in the grander context of fighting for the liberty of future generations. To stir up resentment against the incoming shipments of tea, a revolutionary physician and future signer of the Declaration of Independence, Benjamin Rush, wrote a newspaper article declaring that the "baneful chests" of tea were both a physical and a political poison:

> They contain worse than death—[they contain] the seeds of SLAVERY. Remember, my countrymen, the present era—perhaps the present struggle—will fix the constitution of America forever. Think of your ancestors and think of your posterity.[13]

The Hardest Working Man

John Adams wished he could carry a gun and fight for America's freedom on the battlefield. But as a responsible man, he knew that he had other duties to his country to fulfill. He became probably the hardest working member of the Continental Congress. In the early stages of the War of Independence, he served on nearly one hundred different committees for the Congress.[14] Among other things, he helped to organize the army and its provisions—everything it needed to survive and to fight.

When the war dragged on, America realized it would need the support of the French in order to win. Ben Franklin was already in Paris, the capital of France, befriending the French leaders. Now the Continental Congress asked John to join Ben in the effort to convince the French king to help America's fight against the British king. The French feared and hated the British, but the King of France also worried that America's revolution would spawn other rebellions against authority around the world, including in France.

Even in peacetime, it was miserable and hazardous to take a sailing ship to Europe. But this was wartime. Remember that King George had marked John Adams for death. A British warship could easily have overtaken and captured the boat that was carrying Adams as it slowly made its way across the ocean. If John had been caught, the king would have delighted in hanging him.

The trip took John far away from his beloved wife and children, and his home and farm. He left behind his career as a lawyer to live in a far away country where he couldn't speak the language and where he had no friends or family. He was often sick and at one time became deathly ill, but he continued to expend every bit of energy he could on behalf of his country, negotiating with France and trying to obtain loans from other countries. John Adams would end up spending much of the Revolutionary War alone in Europe pleading the American cause to foreigners.

John's famous letters to his wife Abigail and her letters to him were his only link home. It could take months for these letters to go back and forth on sailing ships, and they could easily get lost or stolen. He couldn't be too personal or share many details of his work for fear the British would intercept his letters. When Adams was still in America at the Continental Congress in Philadelphia, the British had captured some of his letters to his wife in Massachusetts. The letters contained frustrated remarks that John had made about another influential delegate to the Congress. In the hope of stirring up resentment among the rebels, the British published the letters in a hostile newspaper.

Along with Benjamin Franklin and John Jay, John Adams would eventually have the satisfaction of negotiating the Treaty of Paris in 1783 that officially ended the war and formalized British recognition of the United States of America. Then, in one of the more ironic and dramatic turnarounds in history, the king's "most wanted man" became the American ambassador to the king's court. Much has been said about what John Adams must have felt as the American ambassador being formally introduced to King George III—the man who had in the past ordered him to be caught and hanged. It boggles the imagination.

Few men gave as much to their country as John Adams. In 1796 America would recognize his greatness by electing him the second President of the United States.

The First Big Battle

When the American colonists continued to defy the king, the British filled Boston harbor with ships and landed an army of Redcoats that was much larger than the garrison the mob had attacked. In 1775 they took over Boston by force—making that year a turning point in American history and eventually in world history.

King George figured that the worst "hotheads"—the ones who were calling loudest for independence—lived in Boston. One was John Adams and another was John's cousin, Samuel Adams, who was known as a firebrand—an organizer and orator who was actively stirring up rebellion. Samuel had been a leader in the Boston Tea Party. By taking over Boston, the king hoped to stop the rebellion dead in its tracks.

During this time, John Adams, Samuel Adams, John Hancock, George Washington, and many other Founders were gathered in Philadelphia trying to agree on how far they should take their demands for independence from Great Britain. The idea of an army was in the early stages. The Founders did not name it the "American" army because they still hesitated to declare themselves completely independent. They still hoped to work it out with their king. That's why the Founders called their meetings in Philadelphia the Continental Congress and why they called their new army the Continental Army.

When the British army and navy took over Boston, the people of Massachusetts reacted with outrage. They formed their own patchwork army made up almost entirely of local volunteers from their state. Then they surrounded Boston to keep the British from breaking out of the city into the countryside. They were a disorganized bunch of men and boys; but they would help to determine the future of everyone alive today, especially the right to live in a free country where we can choose to become responsible citizens. The armed band of Massachusetts colonists was so undisciplined, and so untrained and inexperienced, that they seemed no match for the soldiers of the British Empire.

The Americans dug trenches into a hill overlooking Boston and then the British attacked their positions in the famous Battle of Bunker Hill, which actually took place mostly on nearby Breed's Hill. The British were sure the Americans would turn tail and run in disarray when a real army bombarded them with cannon and then came charging up the hill looking as unstoppable as the Empire itself.

Two days earlier on June 15, 1775, the Continental Congress had elected George Washington commander-in-chief, but he was still in Philadelphia. There was no single heroic figure to lead the makeshift army. But the colonists knew they were fighting for freedom and that gave them energy and courage. Historian Barry Strauss made the same observations about the people of antiquity when he noted that "democracy energized Athens" in war.[15] He quoted the ancient Greek historian Herodotus:

> When the Athenians lived under a tyranny they were no better at war than any of their neighbors, but after they got rid of the tyrants they were the first by far. This proves that when they were oppressed they fought badly on purpose as if they were slaving away for a master, but after they were liberated they each were eager to get the job done for his own sake.[16]

It also helped that the colonists were such a hardy lot. They might not be trained in warfare, but as farmers they knew how to use the tools of the military trade, including shovels and picks to dig trenches. Many were carrying guns that they had been firing since childhood. Most important, they were fighting for inspired ideals.

Although the country was not yet committed to seeking complete independence from the mother country,[17] the Americans were defending their homes and their freedom, and to some degree the growing idea of liberty itself, for themselves and for posterity. They were volunteers who thought of themselves as citizens, not as professional soldiers. The Redcoats were professionals who were taking orders from and defending the power of King George III—who was very far away across an ocean on an island off the coast of Europe.

With their smug British commanders determined to prove how easily they could overwhelm the inexperienced and untrained Americans, the Redcoats charged up Breed's Hill. The colonists stood their ground and held their fire until by some reports the Redcoats were no more than fifty yards away.[18] Withering fire from the Americans mowed down the oncoming troops and drove them back down the hill. Prodded by the swords of their officers, the British stormed the hill again in second and third waves that were driven back.

The British force had landed 2,400 men at the foot of the hill. They reported losing a huge percentage of their forces: 1,054 casualties with 226 killed on the slopes. Many more Redcoats would die of their wounds. The Americans suffered 441 killed or wounded.[19] As the Americans ran out of ammunition, the British eventually overran their positions; but most of the colonists were able to escape. The British viewed the battle as a horrendous, demoralizing defeat, and the Americans took heart from it.

The lessons of Lexington and Concord, and now Bunker Hill, made the British less confident and more cautious. They had been badly bruised by men firing from behind rocks and trees at Lexington and Concord and they had been slaughtered during a frontal assault on Breed's Hill. They never again tried to fight their way out of Boston, and throughout the war they avoided venturing out of cities into the countryside. They also hesitated to make further frontal assaults against fortified American positions. The eventual result would be a slowly fought, long, and tedious war.

Historian Samuel Griffith II from
The War for American Independence [20]

In the redoubt [the Breed's Hill defenses], officers and sergeants talked to their men in hushed voices: "Fire low"; "Aim at the waist bands"; "Shoot the officers"; "Wait until you see the whites of their eyes"; "Aim at the handsome coats"; "Aim at the commanders." The Americans held fire until the British were less than fifteen rods [less than 250 feet] from the redoubt. Then, suddenly, within ninety seconds, three successive sheets of flame blazed from the parapets. The Redcoats faltered, turned, and stumbled down the hill to the safety of the beach. Again they tried; again they were driven back.

Despite the bloodshed at Concord and Lexington, and now on Breed's Hill, many Americans continued to favor reconciliation. Congress remained reluctant to declare independence and to unleash an all-out war. In the words of historian Robert Middlekauff:

> Still Congress held back from declaring independence. It was waiting for unmistakable evidence that the American people favored a permanent separation. And it hesitated to act while a remnant of the membership retained

> hope that negotiations that might heal the wounds of the last year were possible.[21]

For the moment, there was a stalemate. America's Declaration of Independence was still more than a year away. American independence and the fulfillment of the idea of liberty remained a possibility—but only a possibility. If you had been there trying to figure out who had the power to win a prolonged war between the colonists and the British, you might have picked the Empire.

ABIGAIL ADAMS: AN AMERICAN WOMAN

Colonial Americans were incredibly independent and responsible. Many bravely undertook the hardships of a protracted war. No one exemplified this more than Abigail Adams, the wife of John Adams. Abigail was probably at least as intelligent as John and she helped him think through his most important decisions. When he was away in Philadelphia, and later when he went to Europe to find help in fighting against King George, she managed and took care of everything and everyone that he left behind. Year after year, Abigail had to be a farmer, homemaker, and mother to their children.

The wives of some colonial leaders lived in relative safety while their husbands were away at the Continental Congress in Philadelphia, but Abigail lived near the front lines. John and Abigail owned a farm in Braintree so close to Boston that Abigail huddled with her fearful children in their home listening to the heavy cannon firing when the British stormed Breed's Hill. She wrote her husband, "The constant roar of the cannon is so distressing that we cannot eat, drink or sleep...ten thousand reports are passing vague and uncertain as the wind."[22]

If the British had broken out of Boston, they would have quickly and easily overrun Braintree. Adams had left his wife with the warning, "In case of real danger, fly to the woods with our children."[23] Among her four children, she would have been dragging along a toddler into the forest.

Joseph Warren, the doctor who took care of the Adams family, was a dear friend and a patriot. He was killed at the Battle of Bunker Hill—one of first Americans to die for our independence. His loss was an enormous blow to Abigail, who wrote her husband about the tragedy, bolstering her resolve with verses from the Old Testament, "The God of Israel is he that giveth strength and power unto his people. Trust in him at all times, ye people, pour out your hearts before him..." Her husband wrote back that she was a "heroine."[24]

As a woman of principle, Abigail took a firmer position on slavery than her husband. John, for example, opposed permitting African Americans to serve in the Continental Army and as an attorney he defended slave owners against their slaves. Abigail more openly and adamantly opposed slavery. Probably under her influence, the Adams did not use slaves on their farm even when it would have profited them.

Historian John Ferling from *Setting the World Ablaze*[25]

[John Adams] was married to a woman who denounced slavery as an unchristian abomination, and who wrote her husband in tones that suggested she believed he shared her outlook. Furthermore, John and Abigail, unlike many of their affluent friends in Massachusetts, refused to own slaves, even though bondsmen would have provided more economical labor than the free workers they used on their small farm.

When John was away in Philadelphia meeting with the other Founders, Abigail wrote to him that women ought to have more to say in politics since they often had to bear the hardships of war. She had a profound sense of right and wrong, was often way ahead of her time, and voiced her opinions without compromising them.

John and Abigail Adams represented the best of the American colonists and future citizens of the United States of America. John did as much as anyone to shepherd the nation through the first trying years and he could not have done it without Abigail. John and Abigail are American role models for how to guide our lives by freedom, responsibility, gratitude, and love. I believe that both John and Abigail would have endorsed The Primary Principles as guidelines for living our personal as well as our political lives:

The Primary Principles
Protect freedom.
Take responsibility at all times.
Express gratitude for every gift and opportunity.
Become a source of love.

Chapter Three

Our Declaration to the World About Freedom

Imagine yourself as a successful professional or businessman. You may be a doctor or lawyer; you may own ships or a large farm; you may have inherited wealth or made a sizeable fortune for yourself. You are very well off. This describes the great majority of the Founders.

Beyond success in your work, you have a big family, a beautiful and perhaps palatial home, and a good life. You are highly respected by the people in your community and may even be among the richest and best known citizens in your part of the country. You have everything to lose, and nothing to gain, by doing anything that could shake up or destroy the security of your well-established life. This, too, describes most of the Founders.

Your life is so busy and satisfying that you don't have much reason or motivation to take difficult trips far away from your family and your work. Besides, you are very attached to your local community and to your colony, and you do not strongly identify yourself with America as a whole. You probably think of yourself more as a Virginian or a New Yorker than an American.

Given who you are and the quality of your life, you certainly would not want to risk everything you have—your wealth and property, your reputation, your freedom, and even your life and the lives of your family in order to create a new nation and to fight for its freedom. If you were the wife of one of these men, you probably would not want him to uproot and put at risk your entire family life.

Life was good in colonial America. Why risk unleashing the forces of utter destruction—a civil war between those colonists who supported the king and those who did not, and an international war against the British Empire?

Yet this is exactly what transpired. The United States of America exists today and we have our freedoms because a group of very successful men, supported by their wives, decided to risk everything for their ideals and for the future of you and me, and every other American, and even the world. They came together under the most difficult conditions and signed a document that made them enemies to their king and exposed them to being hanged as traitors. Then they fought a civil war against the king's supporters within the colonies while they went to war against King George III, the mighty British Empire, and the most feared army and navy in the world.

Why would successful men, with the backing of their families, risk everything by signing a document that turned them overnight into criminals with prices on their heads? Why would they endanger everything they had worked for and everyone they loved? That's a lot of what this book is about—how and why people devote their lives to freedom, responsibility, gratitude and love, including love for higher ideals such as liberty, patriotism, and God. Now let's learn about the document that they signed.

PUTTING IT IN WRITING

On July 2, 1776, the delegates to the Continental Congress approved a resolution by Virginian Richard Henry Lee that transformed their lives and eventually the lives of everyone on Earth:

> That these United Colonies are, and ought to be, free and independent States, that they are absolved from all allegiance to the British Crown, and that all political connection between them and the State of Great Britain is, and ought to be, totally dissolved.

This was the day that John Adams thought Americans would celebrate with fireworks forever after. He was wrong about the date only because no one anticipated the incredible power of the document that was soon to follow.

To show that they were united in demanding their freedom, and to explain their reasons to the world, the Founders had already formed a committee to write what became the Declaration of Independence. The best-known members of the small committee were John Adams, Ben Franklin, and Thomas Jefferson. John was too busy and Ben was from an older generation. So Jefferson was selected to do the actual writing. Although very shy in public, and afraid to speak in front of groups, Jefferson was very eloquent with his pen. He wrote words that helped change the world when he confirmed each and every person's "unalienable rights to life, liberty and the pursuit of happiness." He further declared that the purpose of government was to secure or to preserve these rights. Here are the most famous of Jefferson's words—words that you and I can use to guide our lives:

> We hold these truths to be self-evident, that all men are created equal, that they are endowed by their Creator with certain Unalienable Rights, that among these, are Life, Liberty, and the pursuit of Happiness – That, to secure these rights, Governments are instituted among Men, deriving their just Powers from the consent of the governed.

By "unalienable," Jefferson meant that no one could take away these rights. God the Creator grants these rights to us as individuals, they are part of our human nature, and therefore they remain always and forever ours. Those words and the idea behind them have inspired hundreds of millions of people to believe in their right to be free.

In Congress, July 4, 1776

The opening words of the *The Unanimous Declaration of the Thirteen United States of America*

When in the Course of human events, it becomes necessary for one people to dissolve the political bands which have connected them with another, and to assume among the powers of the earth, the separate and equal station which the Laws of Nature and Nature's God entitle them, a decent respect for the opinions of mankind requires they should declare the causes which impel them to the separateness.

When you read the Declaration of Independence, you will find two opinions stated in no uncertain terms: the king was so oppressive that the colonists had the right to separate from him, and that all people have the right to be free to determine the course of their own lives. These words have helped to build an America where you can be free, and they have continued to inspire and to embolden people around the world.

It's worth summarizing the momentous process that brought us our Declaration of Independence. With occasional editorial input from Franklin and Adams, it had taken Jefferson about seventeen days to write this awe-inspiring document. After the Congress approved the Lee Resolution on July 2nd, declaring independence from Great Britain, the much more lengthy Jefferson declaration was then presented to the delegates. It was debated and edited for two days, and then approved on July 4,

1776—the day we celebrate our independence. At that time it was signed by John Hancock, the president of the Congress, and by Charles Thomason, the secretary.

Copies of the Declaration of Independence were immediately distributed throughout the colonies, including to commanding officers of the Continental troops. On August 2, 1776, a freshly minted copy was once again signed by Hancock with his huge, defiant flourish and then one-by-one by most of the other delegates.[26] The atmosphere was sober and determined, and not celebratory. Each man knew that he was committing himself, his family, and his fellow citizens to a potentially ruinous and bloody end.

The Declaration of Independence inspired Americans and jumpstarted the revolution. Copies were read aloud amid noisy celebrations of fireworks and gunfire that set the precedent for modern 4th of July celebrations. Because he was away at war, George Washington had missed the opportunity to sign the Declaration, and now he ordered it read aloud to his assembled troops.

Probably as much as at any time in American history, Americans now believed they were fighting for something much greater than themselves and even greater than their own liberation. The Cause was no longer confined to the defense of their homes and their own personal freedom, or even their newborn nation. They were now aware they were doing something that had never been done before—something that mattered in the history of human beings. They were carrying the new torch of human rights and liberty for themselves and for the world, now and in the future.

A long, bitter war would follow in which General Washington fought mostly defensive actions against superior forces. It would be more than five years before the final battle at Yorktown, Virginia, in October 1781 that led to the surrender of a large portion of the British army. Then it would be yet another year and a half before King George would declare an official end to the fighting, and still longer for peace treaties to be signed in 1783.

Putting Their Lives and Fortunes At Risk

When the Founders signed the Declaration of Independence in the summer of 1776, they knew they were risking their lives. Today we view the fifty-six names on the Declaration of Independence as a roll call of great heroes. We feel respect and gratitude toward our forefathers who courageously signed this document and then took up arms. But to the King of England and his Parliament, the names on the Declaration of Independence made a convenient list of the worst criminals and traitors in the entire Empire. It was a shopping list of people to hunt down and to kill. And indeed, the British would try to do just that, at times sending landing parties and cavalry to try to seize a Founder and his family, or to destroy their home.

The Founders knew that their names might someday be read aloud as the British hanged them one by one. The drama, the dedication, and the risk ring out in the closing line of the Declaration of Independence:

> And for the support of this Declaration, with a firm reliance on the protection of Divine Providence, we mutually pledge to each other our Lives, our Fortunes, and our sacred Honor.

As John Adams put it, "Sink or swim, live or die, survive or perish," he would side with his country against Great Britain.[27] The Founders and their wives and families risked their lives and their fortunes not only because they wanted to be free—but also because they believed in the independence of their nation and in the right of all humanity to be free.

Taking God Seriously

The reference to Divine Providence in the final words of the Declaration of Independence was much more than mere lip service to religion. There was no hypocrisy in their "firm reliance on the protection of Divine Providence." We shall find that the Founders as a group were convinced that their success depended on God. After the war was won, men like George Washington, John and Samuel Adams, and Benjamin Franklin would repeatedly express their gratitude to God for the outcome.

In private letters from Philadelphia to his wife Elizabeth in Boston—personal communications in which he could express his most heartfelt convictions—Founder Samuel Adams told his wife that the future of the nation lay in the hands of God. During this period leading up to the signing of the Declaration of Independence, he sometimes sounded resigned to whatever God would cause to happen:

> I am fully satisfied in the Justice of our Cause, that I can confidently as well as devoutly pray, that the righteous Disposer of all things would [bring success to] our Enterprises. If he suffers us to be defeated in any or all of them I shall believe it to be for the most wise and gracious Purposes and shall heartily acquiesce in the Divine Disposal.[28]

In other letters to his wife, he was more optimistic for the country's success, if not for his own survival; but God remained the final arbiter of what would happen:

> Righteous Heaven will surely smile on a Cause so righteous as ours is, and our Country, if it does its Duty will see an End to its Oppressions. Whether I shall live to rejoice with the Friends of Liberty and Virtue, my fel-

> low Laborers in the Common Cause, is a Matter of no Consequence. I will endeavor by Gods Assistance, to act my little part well—to approve my self to Him, and trust every thing which concerns me to his all-gracious Providence.[29]

This combined theme of trusting in God while taking full personal responsibility resounds throughout the lives of the Founders. They sought God's goodwill and expressed gratitude for it, while they exerted their own will with all their might. It is an ideal formula for how to live one's life and undoubtedly sustained the signers throughout the embattled years to come.

Sam Adams made these communications in letters that also expressed love for his wife. While away at the Continental Congress in June 1775 he wrote to her, "It is painful to me to be absent from you." Later in October he wrote, "My dear Betsy, I have not received a letter from you, altho' it is more than seven Weeks since I left you. ... Pray, my dear, let me hear from you soon. I am greatly concerned for your Security & happiness, and that of my Family."[30]

The letters of Samuel Adams, with their loving devotion to his wife, exemplify the four principles that weave through the lives of the Founders: freedom, responsibility, gratitude, and love. Samuel Adams expressed and embodied all of them.

Like John and Abigail Adams and George Washington, Samuel Adams was a remarkable inspiration for how to live by The Primary Principles:

THE PRIMARY PRINCIPLES
Protect freedom.
Take responsibility at all times.
Express gratitude for every gift and opportunity.
Become a source of love.

The Signers Never Compromised Themselves or Their Cause

From Congressional approval of the Declaration of Independence in July of 1776 until the signing of the treaty of Paris in September 1783, ending the war with Britain, there was seldom much cause for hope and often much reason for fear in the lives of the Founders and their wives and children. Yet not a single one of the fifty-six signers or their wives ever had a change of heart and reneged. Not a single one said, "I've had enough! I've changed my mind, I'm going to support my king, and if necessary I'll flee to England." Thousands of other Americans made that decision—but not one of the Founding fathers and mothers.

T. R. Fehrenbach, from *Greatness to Spare*[31]

Most were offered immunity, freedom, rewards, their property, or the lives and release of loved ones to break their pledged word or to take the King's protection. Their fortunes were forfeit, but their honor was not. No signer defected, or changed his stand, throughout the darkest hours. Their honor, like the nation, remained intact.

Even when the Redcoats were winning most of the battles; even when they occupied our largest cities like Boston, New York, and Philadelphia; and even when the British frontlines were never far distant—not one of the signers crossed over to them. Even when their homes were burned and sacked, they did not reject the great Cause of liberty. All the signers of the Declaration of Independence stayed true to their "mutual pledge" of "our Lives, our Fortunes, and our sacred Honor."

This document was charged with energy, it lived in the hearts and minds of ordinary colonists and revolutionary soldiers, and it changed the world forever. The Declaration of Independence can be a living part of what's best in our lives.

How Much Did The Signers Sacrifice for Us?

In appreciation of how much the Founders have given to us, and to inspire ourselves, we need to recognize how much they sacrificed for us. We know that John Adams, Franklin, and Washington endured grave dangers and lengthy times away from home and family. Washington shared much of the hardship of war with his soldiers, including cruel winters in camp, for many years on end. As we will learn, he repeatedly risked his life leading his troops. Meanwhile, his wife would spend an average of six months with him during the winters when armies on both sides were encamped.

John and Abigail Adams were separated for a total of almost six years while John was representing the United States in Europe; and Abigail was left to manage the farm and to raise the family. John suffered life threatening storms at sea, bitter political disappointments, and almost died alone in Europe.

We know that none of the signers became war profiteers—that is, they did not benefit financially but lost money and wealth as a result of the fighting. Washington even refused to take a salary as Commander-in-Chief. We know that all of them sacrificed a considerable portion of their incomes and, in the case of wealthier men like Franklin and Washington, they sacrificed portions of their fortunes.

As a group, the men who signed the Declaration of Independence had a great deal to lose. Many had inherited wealth, and a number of them had built their own fortunes. As mentioned earlier, they included lawyers, doctors, businessmen, and planters. The richest men in America were among the signers. With the notable exception of Samuel Adams, nearly all of them owned significant property. All seemed to have suffered economically during the revolution, some were wiped out financially, and none is known to have benefited financially after signing the Declaration of Independence. They were not driven as much by self-interest as by principle.

But these brief descriptions of financial hardship do not capture the suffering that the war inflicted on many American patriots and their families. The Revolutionary War was also our first great Civil War in which Americans hated and fought each other. The American Revolution was unlike modern wars where our soldiers have gone off to fight across the ocean, knowing that their families were safe at home. The men who wrote their names on the Declaration of Independence not only signed their own potential death warrants, they put their homes and families in serious jeopardy, not only from the British but from the American sympathizers called Tories or loyalists. As the war dragged on, the fire of patriotism lost its glow for many people. It was often difficult to determine the sympathies of your neighbors and whether or not they could be trusted.

Many colonists did not want to rebel against the king; they thought it was wrong and they thought it was doomed. They resented being forced into an unwanted war by people who did not speak for them. Some fought on the side of Great Britain. Within the colonies, families on both sides of the conflict treated each other very harshly and even violently. Many of the signers of the Declaration of Independence were hounded not only by British troops but also by their neighbors. A neighbor could report your location to the Redcoats or stir up mob violence against you and your family.

The British were brutal toward prisoners, locking up many in vile prison ships where they suffered and died in great numbers of malnutrition, disease, and neglect. Two sons of signer Abraham Clark of New Jersey "took up arms and were captured. They were for a time incarcerated in the Jersey prison-ship, and suffered all the horrors of that confinement until released by a final exchange of prisoners."[32] One can barely imagine not only their suffering but also the anguish of their father and mother during their imprisonment.

Nine of the signers died of "wounds or hardships," five were captured or imprisoned, twelve had homes burned to the ground and seventeen "lost everything they owned." In the words of T. R. Fehrenbach, "What did their act of courage and patriotism get the Signers? At the end, Love and honor remained. The nation remained, too. That was all most of them asked."[33]

The Families of Signers Suffered the Most

The wives and children of the signers often suffered the most. Remember how John Adams warned Abigail to flee with their children into the woods if the British came marching up their road from nearby Boston? Ironically, Benjamin Franklin's wife, Deborah Read Franklin, almost came to harm at the hands of early American revolutionaries who mistakenly thought her husband had betrayed them. She was left alone much of the time while the revolutionary fervor built up. Ben was away at work in London in 1765 when the British passed the hated Stamp Act and some Americans accused Franklin in his absence of advocating the tax. Deborah sent their daughter away for safety but determined to defend their home by herself if necessary. She armed herself and prepared to fend off an assault on her home. Fortunately, a large group of friends came to her defense and frightened off the mob.

After the war began, many wives had to flee their imperiled homes with their terrified children. Some of these women died from imprisonment, exposure to the weather, and stress. Many Native American tribes sided with the British and attacked the colonists, making life near the frontiers hazardous and terrifying for families, especially when the men were away at war.

Letter from Deborah Franklin to her husband Benjamin, 1765[34]

Toward night I said he [cousin Davenport] should fetch a gun or two, as we had none. I sent to ask my brother to come and bring his gun. Also we made one room the magazine. I ordered some sort of defense upstairs as I could manage myself. I said when I was advised to remove that I was very sure you had done nothing to hurt anybody, nor I had not given any offense to any person at all. Nor would I be made uneasy by anybody. Nor would I stir.

The frontier was not far away from the big cities. The biggest battle between the Continental Army and the British-led Indians in New York State took place in the summer of 1779 at Newtown, now called Elmira—nowadays a four-hour drive from midtown Manhattan.

Where I now live in the Finger Lakes Region of central New York State was once deep within Indian country. Elmira is an hour's drive south of Ithaca where I have my office. A little further to the northeast of Ithaca, a notorious massacre by the Indians and British took place at the village of Cherry Valley, near Cooperstown.[35] Descriptions of the horror perpetrated upon women and children are unsuitable for this book.

The area surrounding where I live in the country was once a thriving Cayuga Indian community living beside the beautiful Finger Lake of the same name. In retaliation for attacks on settlers, George Washington ordered the whole area to be ravaged by American troops. Crops, expansive peach orchards, livestock, and whole villages were destroyed; and the Native American inhabitants were forced to flee to Canada.

Signer Thomas McKean wrote to John Adams during the war:

> I have had my full share of the anxieties, cares, and trouble of the present war. ... The consequence was, to be hunted like a fox by the enemy, and envied by those who ought to have been my friends. I was compelled to remove my family five times in a few months, and at last fixed them in a little log house on the banks of the Susquehanna, more than a hundred miles from this place; but safety was not to be found there, for they were soon obliged to move again on account of the incursions of the Indians.[36]

The suffering that the Founding Families endured makes it even more admirable that no signer or signer's wife ever expressed regret over standing up for liberty and country. When signer George Walton thought he was dying from his wounds in a British prison, he wrote to his wife Dorothy, "Remember that you are the beloved wife of one who has made honour and reputation the ruling motive in every action of his life."[37]

Harry Clinton Green and Mary Wolcott Green from *The Pioneer Mothers of America*[38] wrote of the hardships:

> A devoted band of patriotic women who shared the outlawry their husbands had brought upon themselves by declaring their independence of British rule—many of them suffered bitter persecution from British and Tories [British sympathizers]—Mary Bartlett forced to fly with

> her family from her burning home—Elizabeth Adams compelled to resort to needlework to support her family—Elizabeth Lewis imprisoned for months, suffered privations and hardships that led to her death—Mary Morris (N. Y.) driven from a beautiful home, wantonly devastated—Annis Stockton, a homeless refugee after the British looted and burned her home—Deborah Hart, driven from her home, saw her husband hunted for months as a criminal and came to her own death from exposure and anxiety.

Not Always So

Listening to how the early Americans treasured their freedom, and how much we take it for granted today, you could easily imagine that people have always had ideas about wanting to be free. I suspect that people through the ages have experienced stirrings of personal and political independence, but often in vague and voiceless ways.

To yearn for freedom and personal responsibility is part of what we call human nature. Human nature refers to what's built into us as human beings—how we have been made. The Founders believed that we are created by God and by nature to be free and independent, and to be responsible for ourselves. Some of the Founders put more emphasis on God and others on nature—the Declaration of Independence speaks of "the Laws of Nature and Nature's God"—but they all agreed that our basic rights are built into our very being.

Yes, people may have always harbored secret wishes to be free and independent. But while they have wished in their hearts for freedom, they have not always had the idea in their heads. Before our Declaration of Independence and our War of Independence, most people probably did not have the words for their desire to be free and to take charge of their own lives. They didn't have enough experience with freedom to think about it clearly. They had never seen nor heard of a nation that actually fought and won its freedom, and in which human rights were respected and protected. Remember, nowhere in the world at that time could a child or an adult wake up and say, "Wow, I'm an American!" Even today, many nations in the world actively suppress the ideas of freedom and personal responsibility for one's own life, while imposing severe restrictions upon their citizens.

This is important for every one of us to remember all the time. The idea of freedom that the Founders proclaimed to the world more than two hundred years ago is still struggling to gain ground around that world—and not everyone as yet believes in it. Many people don't know about or don't dare to express their basic human rights.

So where did these ideas about freedom and human rights come from? And why did they come to a crescendo in America during the build up to the War of Independence?

Chapter Four

Who Made Up These Ideas About Liberty?

When we were children, we didn't think much about the houses that we lived in with our parents and siblings. We didn't wonder how old the house was, whose idea it was to build it, who designed it, and how much time, effort, and money was required to construct it. Instead, we took the house for granted—it was there for us to live in and to enjoy.

As we got a little older, we thought the same way about ideas like freedom and democracy, and about the government that we lived under. We didn't ask ourselves, "How old are these ideas? Who came up with them? Who worked on them over the years? How much effort and risk did it take? How much does it cost to keep these ideas alive? Has it been worth it?"

Unlike children, adults cannot usually afford to take their homes—or their government—for granted. Without our attention, our home and government alike are likely to go into disrepair, eventually requiring emergency repairs and even major renovations. That's where we are today with our government.

Too many Americans take for granted the ideals of freedom and democracy. Perhaps it's because we no longer see the need to take care of them or to pay for them. We're in a crisis right now with the government taking more and more power for itself, but surprisingly few people see it as a threat to our basic rights and freedom—to the very structure of our political house and home.

They are more concerned about their safety and security in difficult times.

The ideas of freedom and democracy have been growing for thousands of years, sometimes appearing in one place, sometimes in another, and along the way they have changed and grown. We are blessed because these ideas came together in such a special way in the minds and hearts of the Founders and other colonial Americans. We should never, never take these ideas for granted.

I live in a beautiful house overlooking a lake. It is a dream come true in my older years. I know whose idea gave birth to this house. I have met the original owner, seen the original plans and I have some idea about what went into building it. I even know who pioneered the road that I live on and I went fishing with his elderly son before he passed on in his eighties.

My friend had been fishing the lake for more than seventy-five years. Sometimes he used a very old fishing method called jigging in which he bounced minnow-shaped lead weights along the bottom in deep water. Each weight had a hook embedded in it and that crude lure caused the fish to strike. One spring morning we caught our limit of giant Lake Trout in less than an hour.

When I awaken each day with the woods and blue water outside my windows, I almost always think to myself, "I live in a wonderful house." I almost always go to the windows to look out on the woods and water before I begin the morning routine. Not all of us get to live in houses that we love, although with hard work, many can afford wonderful homes. But all of us can wake up in the morning thinking to ourselves, "Wow, I live in America!" Because of the ideas and plans that went into it, America is the most wonderful structure that anyone has ever lived in.

Made In God's Image

Before they took root in America, ideas of freedom, human rights, and democracy had been growing for a very long time. The Hebrew Bible—Christians call it the Old Testament—told the world that God made human beings "in His own image." This inspired people to believe that they have sacred qualities instilled in them by God. If you are a reflection of God—then your rights should be respected. You are a spiritual treasure because God has made you in His image.

In making us in His likeness, God planted within us the yearning for freedom. The Bible dramatizes this passion for freedom in the story called Exodus that has moved the hearts of people, including our Founders. In this drama, God empowers Moses to lead the Jewish people out of bondage in Egypt to freedom and independence in their Promised Land of Israel. During the escape from Egypt, God parts the Red Sea, allowing the Jews to cross unharmed; but when the Pharaoh's army tries to follow, the sea closes in on his pursuing soldiers, and they are drowned.

The story of Exodus began to be written down more than 2500 years ago. The actual events probably occurred more than 3,000 years ago. The yearning for freedom is very old and very enduring. The story of Exodus was very much alive in colonial America. In researching this book, one of the great surprises for me was how much the Founders drew inspiration from the successful flight of the Jews from slavery to freedom.

Referring to Samuel Adams, who did as much as anyone to inspire the American revolution, historian Ira Stoll observed, "The comparison of the American struggle for freedom to the Jews' exodus from the slavery of Egypt was never far from Adams's mind."[39]

IRA STOLL FROM *SAMUEL ADAMS: A LIFE*[40]

Samuel Adams's inspiring speech at York, delivered at a pivotal moment, when the Congress was losing hope, has been lost in the attic of history. ... But the religious themes he struck in his York Speech—that the Americans were like the biblical Israelites of Exodus, and that God was intervening directly on their side—are essential for understanding the American Revolution. So, too, was the association, in the thanksgiving declaration of 1777, of liberty with virtue and piety. These ideas help explain why the Americans fought on in the revolutionary cause in the face of discouraging setbacks and overwhelming obstacles.

Stoll quotes additional comparisons that Sam Adams made between the oppression of the Hebrews and the oppression of the colonists, including the subjugation of the Jews under the Roman Empire.[41] He concludes, "Adams used this metaphor of the colonists as the children of Israel to motivate others, and his belief in it was a source of strength, comfort, and mission for him."[42] Like many Founders, Samuel Adams was deeply imbued with and freely cited Judeo-Christian beliefs and traditions.

Stoll underscores three important themes of the American Revolution: That the idea of liberty was inspired by God, that God intervened on behalf of the Americans, and that freedom depended upon or required living a moral life. This is integrity—understanding and living life with a consistent set of values and ethics.

In early 1776, Washington forced the British out of Boston by surrounding the city with cannon dragged through hundreds of miles of mountains, snow, and ice—all the way from Fort Ticonderoga in the upper reaches of New York State. Washington had good reason to lead his victorious army into the city, but he left the glory to others and instead remained behind and attended a Sunday sermon conducted by the chaplain of the artillery regiment. The reverend chose Exodus for his text, quoting how the Pharaoh gave up pursuing the Jews, because he realized, "the Lord is fighting for them against the Egyptians."[43]

When the Founders were designing the Great Seal or emblem of the United States, Thomas Jefferson proposed a scene from the Exodus with the Jews being led through the wilderness after their escape from Egypt. Franklin proposed a scene of the Pharaoh being drowned by the Red Sea as he tried to chase after the Jews.[44] Although neither of these design suggestions was used, they reconfirm the importance of the Bible and the story of the Exodus to the most influential Founders.

The Ten Commandments

In the Old Testament, God gives Moses the Ten Commandments to bring to the Jewish people. God promises to lead the Jews to freedom and triumph in new lands, in return for which he demands that they obey his commandments.[45] It is a moral contract—I will liberate you and you will obey my commandments.

God begins His commandments by reminding the Jews that He is the one who freed them from the slavery: "I the Lord am your God who brought you out of the land of Egypt, the house of bondage: You shall have no other Gods besides me." Put simply, I brought you from slavery to liberty—so obey me! It's all about freedom and being grateful to God for it. This theme echoes throughout the words of the Founders.

THE TEN COMMANDMENTS[46]

1. **Do not worship any other God.[47]**
2. **Do not worship idols or other false images of God.**
3. **Do not swear falsely using God's name.**
4. **Do not work on the Sabbath; keep it holy.**
5. **Honor your father and mother.**
6. **Do not commit murder.**
7. **Do not commit adultery.**
8. **Do not steal, cheat, or lie to others.**
9. **Do not give false testimony.**
10. **Do not desire anything that belongs to your neighbors, including any of their possessions and property.[48]**

First written more than two thousand years ago, the Ten Commandments are not perfect by modern ethical standards and some of the additional rules that came with them no longer seem remotely fair or just. For example, slavery is accepted as normal in the Tenth Commandment, which forbids coveting your neighbor's "manservant" or "slave." What's remarkable is the enduring truth contained in the heart and soul of these commandments, and its continued inspiration to hundreds of millions throughout the world.

THE TEN COMMANDMENTS ARE GOD'S BILL OF RIGHTS

The Ten Commandments can be viewed as a divinely ordained Bill of Rights. God retains some rights for Himself and gives others to us. In the first four commandments, God demands His rights. The Jews will worship Him alone. The Jews will not worship any false images. They will not misuse His name and they will observe the Sabbath as His special holy day. These commandments can be viewed as defining man's relationship with God as God requires.

In the fifth commandment, God addresses the rights of parents—that they should be honored. This defines our relationship to our parents.

In the final five commandments, God summarizes the rights of human beings—how God orders us to relate to each other. Here's how your basic human rights are expressed in the last five Commandments:

> You have the right not to be killed or murdered.
> You have the right not to have anyone interfere with the sanctity of your marriage.
> You have the right not to have people steal from you, cheat you, or mislead you.
> You have the right not to have your neighbor lie about you.
> You have the right not to have *any* of your private property jealously desired by your neighbor.

These final five commandments are God's bill of rights for human beings. It's worth repeating that they can also be viewed as defining our relationships to each other. They tell us not to mistreat each other. We should not kill each other, rob and cheat each other, lie about each other, interfere in each other's marriages, or desire each other's belongings and property.

The Ten Commandments tell us to protect life, liberty, and property. These rights are gifts from God—and God expects the recipients of these gifts to handle them responsibly.

Many of the stories and poems in the Old Testament teach people to take responsibility for doing what's right. Being responsible is part of the deal that God made with the Jews—to lead them to freedom and the Promised Land, in return for which they would obey his commandments to live responsible lives. It began with God and the Jews, but we now understand that this arrangement or contract represents an agreement between God and all of humanity.

The Old Testament also speaks about the healing power of God's love and teaches people to take care of each other; but the main emphasis is on obeying God, being responsible, and respecting the rights of others.

The Founders knew that the ideas of freedom and responsibility were woven throughout the Old Testament and they drew encouragement from it. We shall continue to show that when fighting the War of Independence, the Founders often used images from the Old Testament of a God who supported their cause and expected their gratitude.

The Golden Rule

The Golden Rule appears in the Old Testament when the Jews are instructed, "Do not seek revenge or bear a grudge against one of your people but love your neighbor as yourself."[49] The New Testament goes much further in telling us again and again that we should love all people as we love ourselves—all people, even our enemies. According to Jesus, the two most important commandments are to love God and to love each other.

The Golden Rule[50]

From the New Testament

Love the Lord your God with all your heart, and with all your soul, and with all your mind, and with all your strength: this is the first commandment.

The second is this: Love your neighbor as yourself. There is no commandment greater than these.

We are taught that we should love God with all our heart and soul, that God loves each and every one of us, that all people are equal in the eyes of a loving God, and that we should love and treat each other well. The idea that we are made in God's image means that we should respect and love each other. Period!

Blessed are the Poor and the Humble

In the Sermon on the Mount, Jesus taught that the poor and humble have more chance of pleasing God than the rich and the powerful. What an earth-shaking idea this was in a world where Caesar, the Roman Emperor, was all-powerful. The mighty Caesar was a god and the poor were nothing.

The world was changed by the Christian idea that the least among us have as much or more worth in God's eyes as the high and mighty. It set the stage for encouraging human rights and democracy in future generations.

Spoken by Jesus in the Sermon on the Mount during the Roman Empire, these words would inspire the colonists nearly two thousand years later when they lived under yet another Empire, this one ruled by King George III.

The Founders were well aware that ideas of freedom and human rights were rooted in the Old and New Testaments. John Adams was amused to hear some colonists claim that the idea of equality was invented during the American Revolution. He wrote to one of his sons that the principle of equality had originated in the Golden Rule, "Love your neighbor as yourself."[51]

In his later years in a letter to Thomas Jefferson, Adams wrote, "The Ten Commandments and the Sermon on the Mount contain my religion." This combination of the Old and the New Testaments became a strong argument for the freedom, responsibility, and the inherent or God-given equality of all human beings. Called the Judeo-Christian tradition, this became the foundation of the Declaration of Independence, the Constitution of the United States of America and the Bill of Rights—all of which promoted human rights, equality, and democracy.

Religious Freedom

Some Founders like physician Benjamin Rush, a signer of the Declaration of Independence who tended the wounded at Valley Forge, and the Boston rebel Samuel Adams, were devout Christians who guided their daily lives by the teachings of Christ.[52] In the words of his biographer Ira Stoll, "Samuel Adams was the archetype of the religiously passionate American founder, the founder as biblical prophet, an apostle of liberty."[53] John and Abigail Adams were also Christians who found comfort and motivation in their religion. Most Americans were Christians and many of them found encouragement for independence and human rights in their religion.

Other Founders like Washington, Franklin and Jefferson believed in God but did not speak fervently about Christianity or describe Jesus as a personal savior. As we shall continue to document, many—including Washington, Adams, and Franklin as well as Samuel Adams and James Madison—believed that God was active in guiding the outcome of America's War of Independence.

Some historians have argued that many of the Founders were Deists—people who believe that God created the world and then stood back without further interference. In reality, all of the Founders we have met in this book believed that God took an active role in human life and should be shown gratitude for the outcome of the War of Independence and even for the Constitution. We shall find this confirmed again and again.

A person does not have to be religious or to believe in God in order to believe in human rights. Many humanists who root their secular values purely in reason and the study of humankind have been strong advocates of liberty and rights. I am focusing on the Judeo-Christian origins of these beliefs so that you can better understand what motivated and guided the Founders to risk their lives and reputations. If their example inspires you without any religious implications, that is fine. But if their example helps you to believe in a loving God who gives meaning to our lives, that is all to the better.

You may be interested to know that I am Jewish, but that I have also been deeply influenced by the teachings of Jesus. For many years as a young man I did not believe in God, but I'm happy to report those days are over. My wife Ginger is Christian and a mighty moral influence in my life.

To this day, religious freedom means exactly that—freedom. In America, a person is free to believe, or not to believe, in religion and in God. However, there is no doubt that this nation was built on Judeo-Christian principles. Some of the most important Founders—including John and Abigail Adams, George Washington, Benjamin Franklin, Benjamin Rush, Samuel Adams, and James Madison—believed that God's moral principles and even His hand guided the struggle for independence. They also believed that a moral and religious America was required to sustain freedom and responsibility as our way of life.

The Enlightenment

Religion was the major but not the only inspiration for human rights among the American colonists. During the century that America was born, philosophers in Europe began to write about the right of individuals to think for themselves, to make choices, to own property, and to work toward their own betterment. These basic values had evolved within the Judeo-Christian tradition, but also were influenced by classic Greek philosophers, by Greek experiments with democracy, and by ancient Roman philosophers as well.

These new European philosophers of freedom often relied more on common sense, reason, and logic than on religious faith. Some of them examined human attributes, such as the ability to think and to make choices. They concluded that these abilities require freedom and the right to own property for their full expression. They were called moral philosophers and they spoke of "natural rights" based on our human nature and our human capacities. Their conclusions further strengthened the argument for freedom and equality.

However, many people do not realize the degree to which faith in God influenced many of these Enlightenment advocates of freedom. John Locke, the English philosopher, inspired the colonists with An Essay on Human Understanding in which he wrote about human equality and the right to life, liberty, and property. His words echo in the Declaration of Independence and many other American expressions of human rights.

A philosopher, yes; but Locke was no atheist. In the same classic essay in which he promoted human rights, Locke also argued for the existence of God. In a memorable sentence, he declared, "For the visible marks of extraordinary wisdom and power appear so plainly in all the works of creation, that a rational creature who will but seriously reflect on them, cannot miss the discovery of a Deity."[54]

The combined influence of these developments within religion and philosophy would later be called the Enlightenment. Even before being named the Enlightenment, these ideas were strongly influencing the American colonists. But for most ordinary colonists, their deepest inspiration came more directly from the Bible, which was often the only book they regularly read.

Adam Smith

Adam Smith was another moral philosopher who influenced the Founders. Smith lived in Scotland—a part of Great

Britain—and he met for dinner and conversation with Ben Franklin shortly before Franklin returned to America to help lead his country's struggle for independence. As a result of living abroad for many years, Ben Franklin knew some of the most influential people in the world.

Smith was said to have shown Franklin pages from his as yet unpublished book, *The Wealth of Nations*.[55] The extraordinarily influential book was not published until 1776—the same year that the Founders would sign the Declaration of Independence. But Franklin carried Adam Smith's ideas back to America with him. After the book was published, James Madison read it while planning the Constitution.[56]

In *The Wealth of Nations,* Adam Smith applied the idea of freedom to economics—the study of how a nation or society creates wealth and material prosperity. Smith found that people are most productive when they are most free. We call this the free market, the free enterprise system, or capitalism. A free people will produce the most wealth in the form of the best products and services for everybody.

Smith explained how free people compete with each other by offering the best and least expensive goods and services that they can. He wanted government to protect the freedom of individuals to conduct their businesses and to offer their services without undue interference.

The free market isn't only about competition; it's also about cooperation. When people are free to compete with each other, they also find ways to work together, if only out of necessity. Making or building almost anything of value requires contributions from many different people with varied resources and skills. Smith described the "division of labor" through which innumerable people with particular skills could make anything from a simple tool to a complex house or ship.

In a famous illustration, Adam Smith described how many different people and organizations it took to manufacture, deliver, and sell a simple pin. The pin would begin as iron ore in the earth and through many steps the metal would be extracted from the ore, manufactured into the pin, distributed to stores, and sold to customers. Each person who participates in the manufacture and sale of the pin tries to make a profit, and competes with others who are also trying to make a profit; but each person must also work cooperatively with others in order to succeed.

Why is it that competition leads people to cooperate and in the long run provides the maximum benefit to the most people? In addition to more practical explanations, Smith suggested that it was as if an "Invisible Hand" led free people in pursuit of their own private interests to help in the production of wealth from which everyone in society would benefit. Smith saw God's hand in making economic freedom work. Although he mostly used the term "Providence," we shall find that George Washington also specifically spoke of God's Invisible Hand.

Smith observed that the free market could not work unless people dealt fairly and honestly with each other. Lying, stealing, and cheating prevent people from competing honestly with each other and stop them from cooperating. Put another way, unless people agree to obey the Ten Commandments so that they can trust each other, they cannot make the most of freedom. Echoing the Golden Rule, Smith spoke of the importance of "fellow feeling" in controlling the worst aspects of competition.

As already emphasized, the Founders also believed that freedom could not succeed without the support of a moral society. This was one of their major themes—the necessity of a society in which people would "Do unto others as you would have others do unto you."

The idea of "fellow feeling" can be traced back to the concept of the Golden Rule. It can also be traced back to the Ten Commandments, which order us to respect the property of others and not to lie, cheat, and steal in our relationships with our "fellows" or fellow human beings. Without this kind of caring and respectful attitude, freedom cannot survive and society cannot function democratically and with respect for individual rights. The free market cannot function without people trusting each other to abide by their verbal and written agreements or contracts. People must be taught to love one another—or at the least to respect one another—for a free society to function.

The principles behind the free market or free enterprise are the same ideas that make it possible for you and me to live a productive life—a healthy combination of competition and cooperation with other individuals. If we are going to compete in an ethical way with other people, we must never forget that we are competing with individuals who have the same rights as we have to be protected from theft and cheating. The more we are able to create trusting relationships with other people, the more successful we will be.

In economics, as in everything else, human beings need to live by the values of liberty, responsibility, gratitude, and love—The Primary Principles:

The Primary Principles
Protect freedom.
Take responsibility at all times.
Express gratitude for every gift and opportunity.
Become a source of love.

The world will never be a perfect place—or even close to it. People will at times disrespect property and steal, lie and cheat; but we must persist in working together to continually improve society. Similarly, we will never be perfect as individuals but we can strive to be honest with each other at all times. Although hard to put into practice in society and in our own lives, these ethics are necessary both for a healthy national life and for happy and successful individual lives.

We have now looked at the background behind the ideals that motivated the Founders. But why did these ideas take such deep root for the first time in history in colonial America?

Chapter Five

Freedom: Growing Like Butterfly Bushes in America

My wife Ginger loves a plant called the butterfly bush—its flowers attract butterflies all summer long. So, with the help of my carpenter friend Lee, I built a giant wooden box near the road at the top of our steep driveway, filled it with topsoil, and planted three butterfly bushes.

In their first year, the plants grew six or eight feet tall and were covered with white, lavender, and purple flowers. In their first fall, I pruned them back and left the long brown stalks and their dried flowers lying on the roadside. To my disappointment one of the bushes had died—the lavender one—and perhaps as dying plants sometimes do, it "went to seed," leaving behind more hearty or numerous seeds than usual.

It was nearly wintertime and the central New York weather quickly became so cold that I neglected to pick up the cut stalks from the road. The big flower box was near the mailbox and the people who delivered the mail and the newspapers drove their cars over the remains all winter long until they were crushed into nothing.

Butterfly bushes don't easily naturalize in this climate—that is, they don't readily spread on their own. That's why they are expensive to buy as individual plants. But in the spring the miracle of the butterfly bushes occurred. Everywhere that rain and melted snow had run off the road, the butterfly bush seeds had been carried along. Water from the roadway near the wooden planter ran down the driveway, and so the seeds lodged in everything from the rocks lining the driveway to the edges of the drainage grate at the bottom. In the spring, seedlings sprouted on the sides of the driveway and from the drains.

Seeds were also washed down the sloping roadside where they became caught in the gravel on the shoulder of the road. They also sprouted, creating a nearly sixty-foot long butterfly bush hedge. And where I shoveled snow from the driveway that winter and threw it onto the hillside garden, the seeds got stuck around rocks, boulders and terracing, and sprouted all over my garden. Ever since, I've had lavender butterfly bushes, and a few purple and white ones, growing like weeds all over the place.

When freedom started to sprout after being seeded around the colonies, it was as unplanned as the naturalizing of my butterfly bushes. Without anyone structuring it, the conditions were right and the idea of freedom grew.

But then the government intervened—in my garden. As always, the government was trying to be helpful. (I am not making this up.) In the second spring of its life, the long hedge beside the road exploded into life. In the early spring, when it was about two or three feet tall, with a lot of growing left to do, along came the county highway department with its giant mower. The county workmen had never seen a hedge of butterfly bushes. To be honest, before they flower, butterfly bushes resemble huge, scraggily weeds. Thinking they had come upon a dreadful overgrowth of something no one could possibly want, the highway department workers mowed down every last one of my several dozen plants in a row.

At the moment I discovered that my beloved hedge had been raggedly torn off just above the roots, it was like being hit in the pit of my stomach. I was so shocked that I nearly fell to my knees on the road. But guess what happened? I recovered and so did my bushes. They reacted to this violent spring pruning by growing back that very summer, thicker and more beautiful than I originally anticipated.

King George and his British government had never seen freedom sprouting up the way it did—like a defiant hedge up and down the eastern coast of America from New Hampshire to Georgia. Exactly like my hedge looked to the county government workers, the king and his men saw this riotous overgrowth of freedom as a bed of weeds—something that needed to be chopped down or uprooted, the quicker the better, before it spread. The King tried to do just that and—guess what? Like my butterfly bushes, freedom grew back even more vigorously.

Now most of the world knows that freedom is among the most beautiful of all creations. It began as isolated weeds in the American colonies, then grew into beds of wildflowers, and now liberty is being cultivated in places no one ever expected it to take root.

What made colonial America such a great place for freedom to start growing?

Almost Everyone Is Privileged in America

Freedom didn't have much chance to grow in Europe. If you lived in Great Britain instead of colonial America, then your opportunities in life were mostly decided in advance by the status of your family. The king and his royal family, the aristocracy, and the priesthood made up the "privileged" few. Most other people had few if any rights or opportunities. They were thought of as commoners.

If you were born into a noble or privileged family, you were thought to deserve wealth and position, and many opportunities would become available to you. If you were born into poverty, you were thought to deserve little or nothing for yourself, and you and your family would likely remain poor.

These limitations on opportunity largely broke down in the American colonies, at least for free white men. Some of the Founders, most famously Ben Franklin, were "self-made" men. They came from ordinary families but went on to make successful lives for themselves. In Europe, they would have had no chance to grow wealthy or to become leaders as they did in America. Most of the Founders worked hard in their youth to mature into self-reliant adults. They saw a parallel between their own personal maturation and the growing independence of the colonies.

Today many people take for granted the American Dream. They realize that it's harder to be born poor than rich, but they also know that many people have risen from poverty to enormous success, even to the presidency of the United States. As Americans, we assume that we have the opportunity as individuals to become independent and self-directed, and even successful; but this is a relatively new idea in human history. A government that protects our freedom to take charge of our own lives—that idea remains at the heart of being an American.

HISTORIAN JOHN FERLING FROM *SETTING THE WORLD ABLAZE*[57]

As Washington, Adams and Jefferson reached the cusp of adulthood, each exhibited a passion for independence. Each hungered for emancipation from the entanglements of childhood and sought to carve out an autonomous existence. The handmaiden to each young man's zeal for self-mastery was a propulsive ambition that drove him to yearn for more than his father had attained, for more even than his father had ever hoped to achieve.

Let's examine why these ideas of freedom and independence grew so gloriously in America.

Most Americans Could Read

You might imagine that the colonists, mostly a roughneck bunch with little or no formal education, probably didn't do much reading and thinking. You might further imagine that very few people could even read. Nothing could be further from the truth. According to historian Samuel Griffith, "About 90 percent of the adult population of Massachusetts was literate. John Adams wrote that an illiterate man in Massachusetts was 'as rare as a comet.'"[58] (Unfortunately, the high literacy rates depended on excluding slaves from the estimates.) More than most citizens today, ordinary colonists read about politics and even debated the underlying principles or philosophy of government.

The colonies were electric with ideas about freedom and independence. Newspapers and pamphlets created a kind of blogosphere—one made of a blizzard of printed-paper. People read speeches and booklets about liberty and passed them around. Often turning to these pamphlets, and authoring some on their own, ministers gave sermons about liberty from the pulpit on Sundays.

Common Sense, the most influential pamphlet of all, was published in January 1776—about half-a-year before the Declaration of Independence—and its powerful message sparked the smoldering freedom movement into a firestorm. George Washington, his officers, and his men read *Common Sense*. The general said that the pamphlet turned the tide of public opinion toward independence with ringing words like, "The blood of the slain, the weeping voice of nature cries, 'Tis time to part.'" The author was talking about "parting" from the King of Great Britain. He was talking about independence.

The writer was Thomas Paine. He published *Common Sense* anonymously because he feared being hanged for treason. Paine gave away a fortune by donating the royalties to the Continental

Congress to help to support the growing war effort. Overnight his book became a runaway bestseller. Imagine this—in a nation of little more than two million people, half-a-million copies were sold within the first year, enough for one in every four citizens.

I doubt if any group of people has ever been so exposed to one little pamphlet with such profound effects. Everyone was talking about and debating the movement toward independence from the British Empire.

FROM *COMMON SENSE* BY THOMAS PAINE

But Britain is the parent country, say some. Then the more shame upon her conduct. Even brutes do not devour their young; nor savages make war upon their families.... I challenge the warmest advocate for reconciliation, to show, a single advantage that this continent can reap, by being connected with Great Britain. I repeat the challenge, not a single advantage is derived. ... But the injuries and disadvantages we sustain by that connection, are without number; and our duty to mankind at large, as well as to ourselves, instruct us to renounce the alliance.

Benjamin Rush was a friend of Tom Paine, influenced his writing, and suggested the name "Common Sense" for the book. Rush wrote about how deeply the revolution impacted on the minds of every American at the time:

> The revolution interested every inhabitant of the country of both sexes, and of every rank and age that was capable of reflection. An indifferent, neutral spectator of the controversy was scarcely to be found in any of the states.[59]

America's Great Spaces Encouraged Freedom

The Americans were widely spread out among the thirteen colonies, spilling over the frontiers to the west. Relatively few people lived in cities. There was a lot of empty space. People had elbowroom. The frontier was dangerous, but it offered even greater opportunities to independent spirits willing to take the risks.

In 1775 the country was moving toward open rebellion against King George. The Second Continental Congress was meeting in Philadelphia. Remember that the British suffered heavy casualties skirmishing with the local colonists at Lexington and Concord, George Washington was named Commander-in-Chief of the army, and the British were stunned by a bloody battle fought at Breed's Hill on the outskirts of Boston.

Meanwhile, in the same year, America's most famous frontiersman, Daniel Boone, was blazing the Wilderness Road through the Cumberland Gap in the Appalachian Mountains. The West was being opened to further settlement.

Great Britain? Who cared! America was expansive and expanding. There was no holding us back. Hundreds of thousands of people would trek through the Cumberland Gap in the coming years. Boone himself would become famous by fighting Indians who sided with the British during the War of Independence.

So few people in such a great land with so many resources. So much opportunity for the daring. No wonder that Americans became an independent people who valued their freedom.

Great Distance from the King Encouraged Freedom

Long before the great Cause captured the imagination, American colonists were already experiencing how good it felt to be free and independent. And they could already see how well it worked. Meanwhile, they lived so far away from King George that it was hard for them to swallow the idea that he had a right to control their lives. There was nothing like living in a spacious country far away from any other powerful countries to encourage freedom and independence.

Many Americans felt like youngsters nowadays feel when they graduate from high school and move away to college. With Mom and Dad so far away, they want more freedom and independence. They often become angry with their parents and accuse them of still trying to treat them like children. This is how many Americans felt about the king—their "father" and the "mother country" was too far away to exert control over them anymore.

As far as many colonists were concerned, they had left Europe behind—and good riddance. Distance bred contempt and independence.

An Independent People

Conditions demanded that the colonists become a very hardy bunch of men and women. Remember Abigail Adams and how she managed the family farm and the children while her husband was away working for the war effort? Remember how she remained on her farm rather than take flight while the Battle of Bunker Hill was raging within earshot?

Many colonists like the Adams family lived on small farms where they built their own houses, barns, and fences; cleared their own fields and grew their own crops; and tended to their own animals. Imagine cutting down a forest full of trees with saws and axes, and prying up huge rocks, all by hand. Imagine plowing with a horse or, if you had no horse, pulling a plow behind you as if you were the horse. Imagine planting seeds in the springtime and then depending on them to sprout and grow into food to keep you alive through the wintertime. Imagine taking your gun into the woods to defend yourself from Indians while hunting deer and turkey for meat.

These farmers were very self-sufficient. They were as tough as the boulders and tree stumps they dug out of their pastures. Living like that, they had little reason to feel dependent on King George for anything. They saw no reason to pay this fellow George their hard-earned money when he wasn't doing anything for them in return.

Other colonists worked in towns and cities as tradesmen making goods that people needed—books and newspapers, barrels and tools, hats and shoes, carriages, houses, and ships. To earn money and to survive, they had to work hard and to compete with other tradesmen. Or they offered services like shoeing horses, repairing tools, or providing food and lodging. They had to offer a useful service or to make something worthwhile that other people would want to buy. They too felt self-sufficient and proud of their independence. They wanted to be responsible for themselves. Many of Boston's fiery rebels came from this group.

Some colonists lived on the frontier and seldom if ever saw a city or even a large building. If they stayed home throughout the entire War of Independence, they would never hear enemy gunfire. Sometimes they built their farms in valleys surrounded by rugged hills or mountains and fast moving streams and rivers. A few were even more independent. They lived off the land by hunting and by trapping animals for their fur. These men and women hardly had much time to think about a king, let alone to care about what the king thought of them.

As soldiers gathered to fight against Great Britain, one of these "backcountry" companies of men came from the Blue Ridge Mountains of Virginia. Unkempt, with bucktails in their hats and scalping knives or tomahawks in their belts, they looked as savage and dismaying as "wild Indians" to their more civilized contemporaries. And they loved freedom. They wore rough shirts with words like "Liberty or death" imprinted on them. One of their flags showed a rattlesnake, coiled and ready to strike, with the words "Don't Tread on Me!" As historian David Hackett Fischer points out, their use of "Me" indicates how personally these backwoodsmen took their liberty.[60]

Other Americans grew wealthy owning ships and businesses. They resented King George telling them where their ships could sail, what they could carry on them, and with whom they could trade around the world. They hated the king for sending governors to rule their colonies and they wanted to have more freedom to make their own laws. Leaders like John Hancock came from this group.

Slave Owners for Freedom

More than half the signers of the Declaration of Independence owned slaves.[61] Some of the most vocal leaders of the American Revolution had grown rich owning slaves, sometimes hundreds of them, in Maryland, Virginia, North and South Carolina, and Georgia. Some of these rich colonists lived as well or better than royalty, and were sympathetic to King George. Others became so wealthy and powerful that they resented anyone telling them what to do including that same King George.

It's seems ironic and even baffling that the loudest and most convincing voices for freedom came from men like George Washington and Thomas Jefferson, and numerous others, who owned slaves. Many of the leading Founders and greatest voices for liberty came from Virginia where the slave laws and practices were especially harsh. Slaves had no more rights than cows or chickens, and were often treated worse than animals. Slave women frequently were sexually assaulted by their masters. Slave children were almost never taught to read and write, and they could be torn away from their parents and sold to some distant plantation at the whim of the slaveholder.

Founders like Washington and Jefferson admitted that owning slaves made them feel guilty and ashamed. In 1781, as the War of Independence reached a crescendo, Jefferson wrote dismally about how the slaves might someday rebel. He envisioned that a just God in the Old Testament tradition would take sides with the oppressed slaves, and that they would triumph over their white masters. But Jefferson did nothing to live up to his expressed sentiments against slavery.

THOMAS JEFFERSON IN *NOTES FROM VIRGINIA*[62]

Indeed I tremble for my country. When I reflect that God is just: that his justice cannot sleep for ever: that considering numbers, nature and natural means only, a revolution of the wheel of fortune, an exchange of situation, is among possible events; that it may become probable by supernatural interference! The Almighty has no attribute which can take sides with us in such a contest.

The meaning of Jefferson's tortured language in *Notes from Virginia* is clear—Providence will not side with white Americans in this battle. God will intervene on behalf of the slaves.

Nonetheless, Jefferson continued to buy and sell slaves, and to pay rewards for the capture of his escaped slaves, benefiting from the worst aspects of slavery for the remainder of his life. He chose to support his high style of living at the expense of his principles and at grave cost to those he held in bondage, as well as to the future of America.

Because they had slaves to perform the most exhausting, boring, and time-consuming chores, men like Jefferson had extra time to read, think, and write about freedom. Jefferson's library grew so large that he eventually sold it to the government to start the Library of Congress. Perhaps owning slaves made some of these men more acutely aware of the importance of their own freedom. Rebellious colonists frequently spoke of their refusal to be "slaves" of King George. But it remains difficult to understand how men who owned slaves could write some of the most eloquent and compelling statements about freedom and fight so hard for their own freedom while keeping others enslaved.

The British noticed this contradiction between what many Founders said about freedom and how they actually behaved in owning slaves. The British ridiculed Americans for being hypocrites. Samuel Johnson, the famous "Dr. Johnson" of British letters, remarked that the "loudest yelps for liberty" came from slaveholders. Some Founders, including physician and signer Benjamin Rush, were critical of that same hypocrisy.[63]

The ideals of the Founders were at times much better than their behavior. But that's true of every human being and every society—and many of the Founders were very admirable in their personal lives. Some actively opposed slavery throughout their lives, notably Samuel Adams and Benjamin Rush. Rush became a leading abolitionist when this was an extremely unpopular stance.[64] As we saw earlier in the book, John Adams went along with slavery early in his career, although his wife Abigail openly opposed it. We will continue to examine the failure of the Founders to deal honorably with slavery. The Founders left us their inspiring ideals—and their not always so inspired behaviors—and it's up to us to continue working toward a more ideal America, one that conforms ever more closely to its founding principles.

With the election of Barak Obama, our first African-American president, America has taken another giant step forward toward overcoming the tragic legacy of slavery and racism. Although the Founders would criticize and resist President Obama's wholesale promotion of a larger and more interventionist government, the Founders would celebrate an event that many of them thought impossible—A man with an African father holding the highest office of the nation that they created.

Next we will look at the life of George Washington, one of the most responsible men who ever lived, a man whose choices will further help us to understand what it means to be responsible. If Washington had not made the decisions that he made, we might not be able to wake up in the morning thinking, "Wow, I'm an American!"

Chapter Six

George Washington: The Greatest Man Alive

George Washington commanded the Continental Army that won the War of Independence, staying with his soldiers through years of humiliating defeats, bitterly cold winters, and desperate times. He was president of the convention that created the Constitution of the United States of America. He was elected the first President of the United States and made that office into a position of respect and responsibility.

George Washington was easily the most physically courageous Founding Father. He was also the greatest leader among the Founders. Few would disagree.

But as much as Washington should be praised for what he did as a brave soldier and as a great leader, his magnificent character was most fully displayed in his moral restraint—in what he chose not do. During the war, he rarely asserted his own will and instead continually bowed to the authority of the Congress. He always took seriously the advice of his generals before making critical decisions for the army. He was restrained and humane in his treatment of prisoners, even the Hessians who had previously murdered wounded American soldiers.[65] He never took hostages or shot American collaborators, and he did not encourage retaliation against individual Tories or towns who sided with the king. He was a model of moral restraint and demanded the same conduct from his soldiers.[66] After the war, Washington refused to seize power for himself, but instead made sure that

America got a good start as a democracy that focused on preserving and protecting the individual rights of its citizens.

Responsibility means doing what we know is right and not doing what we know is wrong. Responsibility is often displayed with greatest difficulty and therefore most admirably in things we decide not to do, especially when we have the opportunity to take advantage.

Becoming General Washington

John Adams played an important role in selecting George Washington to be Commander-in-Chief of the Continental Army. Remember there were thirteen colonies, and Massachusetts and Virginia were the most influential. John was from Massachusetts and some expected him to favor the selection of a general from his own state. Washington, of course, was from Virginia.

George Washington rarely put himself forward in obvious ways. He was so tall and his appearance so striking that all he had to do was to show up at a meeting in order to command attention and respect. So he must have wanted very much to lead the new army because on the selection day he came dressed in a spectacular uniform that he had made for himself when he was a colonel in the Virginia militia. He was the only man in the room in military uniform. When John Adams made clear that he supported George Washington, the Virginian was quickly chosen to be the commanding general of the new Continental Army.

Washington Refuses to Become King George of America

Having rid itself of one King George, America could easily have ended up with another. As Commander-in-Chief of the victorious army and then as the first President of the United States of America, George Washington was so enormously powerful and so wildly popular that he could have taken anything he wanted for himself. He could have made himself King George of America.

When the War of Independence was over, officers in Washington's army wanted to march on Philadelphia to force the Continental Congress to pay their long overdue back wages. This could have led to a coup—a military take over of the government by soldiers who wanted George Washington to lead the new nation.

Washington's officers met in a church in preparation for marching against the American congress. Washington came to their meeting and spoke to them. He expressed overwhelming disappointment that the men he cherished and respected would turn against the values for which they had fought together so hard and long. He was masterful in expressing his weariness from the war effort and in voicing his sadness over their threatened rebellion. When Washington was done, some of his men were crying, the potential rebellion was over, and a rogue army would not march on Philadelphia to intimidate the fledgling government of our new nation.

When the Revolutionary War was over, some Americans wanted the great general to establish a royal family line to give strength and stability to the new nation. Many already worshiped him as if he were a god. Instead, Washington retired to his plantation home in Mount Vernon, Virginia, and gave the toddler nation a chance to exercise its democratic legs.

Nothing like this had ever before happened in the history of the world. With his adoring army at his back and his equally adoring country at his feet, a triumphant general chose to hand over power to the representatives of the people for the sake of freedom and democracy. Indeed, George Washington felt insulted and outraged at the suggestion that he use the army to make himself king.[67]

Several years later in 1788 during the debate over increasing government power under a new Constitution, a critic of government power warned that the country had been saved by the integrity of General Washington. If Washington had "possessed the spirit of a Julius Caesar," then "the liberties of this country" would have terminated with the conclusion of the war.[68]

WILLIAM J. BENNETT FROM *AMERICA: THE LAST GREAT HOPE*[69]

Washington drove a stake through the heart of monarchy in America: if he would not be king, *nobody* could be king. And that was the end of kingship in America *forever*. America has had forty-three presidents—including some liars, 'lemons,' and losers—but we have never had a tyrant. For that we can thank George Washington.

When asked several years later to run for president of the United States, Washington agreed and was elected without opposition. It would be the only uncontested presidential election in our history. He served for two terms, a total of eight years, and probably could have been re-elected to the presidency for the remainder of his lifetime. Instead, he refused to run for president for a third term, establishing that this new government would be run by the people and by its laws, and not by a single man, however popular or genuinely heroic he might be. Once again, by refusing to take advantage, George Washington used his power and stunning popularity to make sure that America became a democratic nation. He remained a model of responsibility—doing what he knew was right.

George Washington and the U.S. Army Core Values

Although some of my heroes are advocates and practitioners of non-violent resistance like Martin Luther King, Jr. and Mahatma Gandhi, I am not a pacifist. I know that liberty at times must be defended by military power. Recently I addressed a military conference on how to help soldiers deal with stress.[70] I was struck by how the brave men and women of our armed services view themselves as protecting the values we associate with the founding of this nation. They risk injury and death out of love for their country and its values, love for their families and fellow citizens, and love for each other as warriors fighting together on the frontlines.

In boot camp, along with his or her dog tags, every soldier is given a card to carry that lists the seven core Army values: Loyalty, Duty, Respect, Selfless Service, Honor, Integrity, and Personal Courage. According to the army, these values "are our baseline, our foundation, and our core. The moral and ethical tenets of the Army Values characterize the Army culture and describe the ethical standards expected of all Soldiers."[71] George Washington was the first great exemplar of the Army core values that are embedded and expressed in all of our armed services.

Washington Racially Integrates the Army with Black Americans

George Washington integrated black soldiers into the Continental Army. African-American men who had been freed from slavery fought side-by-side, shoulder-to-shoulder, with white soldiers, and at times probably made up between 6 and 12 percent of the army.[72]

Some historians emphasize that Washington was initially reluctant to bring blacks into his fighting force. It was very threatening to his fellow Virginians and other advocates of slavery. These historians explain that Washington was a practical man and that he needed more soldiers to fill up his army, so he reluctantly let freed blacks fight. But practicality doesn't explain why Washington brought blacks into the army ranks as equals.

Later in our history, the United States desperately needed soldiers during the bloody Civil War. But when President Lincoln reluctantly decided to include blacks in the Union army, he segregated them into their own units with white officers. The U. S. also needed soldiers in World War I and in World War II, but never integrated blacks into the ranks. In every war after the War of Independence until the Korean War—if they were allowed to fight at all—blacks never fought side-by-side with whites. They were put into segregated units or into menial roles like kitchen help. American black people were never again so fully integrated in the army until several years after Harry Truman ordered it the 1950s—nearly two hundred years after George Washington initially integrated the Continental Army.[73]

Think of what George Washington did. With the slave states threatening to withdraw from the War of Independence unless slavery was upheld, so that even anti-slavery Founders constantly compromised on the issue—George Washington nonetheless integrated the Continental Army. In the words of historian Joseph Ellis, "Here was a stunning if silent social statement far ahead of popular opinion."[74]

Washington himself was a slaveholder. By integrating the army, he made clear that blacks were trustworthy and capable of fighting for liberty alongside whites. Washington proved something that almost no one at the time, including Thomas Jefferson, wanted to believe—that blacks and whites could live and work together as one, and that blacks could excel. Yes, Washington was a practical man, but much more importantly he lived as best he could by the principles embodied in the Declaration of

Independence, that all men are created equal. He was responsible and tried to do what was right.

Washington's Best Friend?

At the height of the Revolutionary War in 1780, a painting of George Washington by John Trumbull shows the uniformed general standing alone in an elegant pose. Only one other figure emerges from the background of the painting—William Lee, who was Washington's friend and close companion on the battlefield. As an indication of his status, Lee sits astride a horse.[75] It is astonishing to consider that he was Washington's slave.

In another famous painting of Washington crossing the Delaware by Thomas Sully, the general sits firmly on his agitated white stallion as a storm gathers behind him. Huddled around him are shadowy figures that represent his fearful staff. Other than Washington himself, only one man is recognizable and seemingly unflustered—the same William Lee who is mounted on a rearing dark horse.[76]

A French engraving from the same year shows Washington holding the Declaration of Independence. An unidentified African American, surely the same William Lee, is again the only other figure who is present. Reflecting his actual role, he is holding a horse.[77]

How much did Washington rely upon William Lee? Throughout the war, Lee rode into battle beside Washington. When the general suffered through the freezing winter with his soldiers at Valley Forge, Lee was with him. When the general risked his life by leading troops straight into the face of heavy enemy gunfire, Lee was often beside him. Washington trusted Lee so much he put him in charge of his treasured personal papers during the military campaigns. He referred to Lee fondly as "my fellow."

According to historian David Hackett Fisher, "William Lee was said to be as fearless as Washington himself..."[78] Lee even helped Washington stop a violent breakdown of order among the troops, one that stemmed in part from racial tensions. Early in the war, many soldiers came from "backcountry"—the least civilized parts of the colonies. They were fiercely independent men who resisted army discipline. They also resented the fancy airs put on by the Virginia "gentlemen" who held commanding roles in the army. Conflicts also broke out between the slave-holding Virginians and the Marblehead, Massachusetts regiment that included former slaves as soldiers.

Finally the quarrels turned into a huge brawl among more than one thousand troops in the army camp. Based on a first-hand account, historian David Hackett Fischer captured these events:

> As the fighting spread through the camp, Washington appeared with his "colored servant, both on horseback." Together the general and William Lee rode straight into the middle of the riot. ... In a few moments George Washington and William Lee had restored order in the army.[79]

After the war, William Lee remained with Washington as a slave at Mount Vernon. The Washington Family portrait by Edward Savage in 1796 shows George Washington, his wife Martha, and Martha's two grandchildren by her first marriage—and a glimpse of a figure attending to the family in the background who is dressed in the colorful livery typically worn by William Lee.[80]

When Washington died three years later in 1799, he freed only one of his slaves, William Lee, and gave him a pension. In his will, Washington acknowledged Lee's "faithful services during the Revolutionary War." Washington's other slaves were not freed by his will until after the death of his wife Martha Washington, which occurred a few years later. By the time William Lee was set free, he suffered from several chronic injuries and he chose to remain at Mount Vernon living on his pension until his death. People would stop by to hear his stories of the war—a legacy that seems lost to us forever. To this day Lee remains a little-known, fascinating, and remarkable person in our history. If he had been a white man, he would have been awarded a prominent place in our history books.

Slavery produced strange and conflicted relationships. Imagine the moral conflict when your closest companion in war and peace is also your slave? Imagine being a slave, and devoting your life to your master, acting as his protector, and fighting for his cause? Washington seemed to have few intimate friends; but William Lee seems like a close and dear friend, tested through years of companionship under unimaginable stresses. Slavery lived on as an unholy compromise between the free and the slave states for many years; and it persisted as an equally unholy compromise within the hearts and lives of many Americans, even George Washington.

In his defense, Washington was much more concerned with implementing fairness and justice toward the slaves than most of the Founders, especially those who owned plantations. In his will Washington not only freed all his slaves on his wife's death, he provided for the care of those who were unable to support themselves. Young freed slaves would be taught to read and trained for a "useful occupation." Under no circumstances were the freed slaves to be forced to leave Virginia, as men like Jefferson had proposed in their "solutions" to the "problem." Historian John Ferling observed that the generous provisions of Washington's will "condemned Mount Vernon to ruin." Ferling suggests that "His will was an act of atonement for a lifetime of concurrence in human exploitation," and that Washington hoped to set an example for other large slaveholders.[81]

WASHINGTON'S HEROISM AND BELIEF IN GOD

It's been said that while men like John Adams went off to Harvard for their educations, George Washington went off to war for his. More than two decades before he took over the Continental Army, Washington was a young colonel in the Virginia militia, where he fought alongside his British commanders against the French and Indians on the frontier.

Unlike today's schools, Washington's remarkable heroism and good fortune in battle was commonly taught to children in past generations. Washington seemed "absolutely fearless" in battle. He wrote to a friend, "who is there that does not rather Envy, than regret a Death that gives birth to Honor & Glorious memory."[82] Still a young man, he confided in his brother Jack, "I heard Bullets whistle and believe me there was something charming in the sound."[83]

Young Washington's experiences in battle on the frontier made him seem bulletproof. He repeatedly put himself ahead of his troops in the line of fire and was never even nicked. In the Battle of Wilderness in Western Pennsylvania in 1755, the French and Indians ambushed Washington's Virginia militiamen and a force of British regulars under General Edward Braddock. With bullets tearing into his horse and even through his clothes, Colonel Washington rallied the troops. When Braddock was mortally wounded, Washington risked his life to rescue the general's body from desecration by the Indians.

Washington would fight at the front of his frightened troops while they took cover behind him. The Indian chief in the Battle of the Wilderness decided that "the Great Spirit" protected the tall officer who rode on horseback in plain sight while the Indians fired at him repeatedly without hitting him. Washington seems to have drawn the same conclusion—that he fought under God's protection.[85]

Historian Peter Henriques from *Realistic Visionary*[84]

George Washington came close to losing his own life as well. During [the Battle of Wilderness], he had two or three horses shot from under him (reports vary) and received four bullet holes in his clothes, one of them through his hat. In his words, "Death was leveling my companions on every side of me," but neither then nor later did a bullet ever pierce his skin, giving rise to stories among the Indians and others that he was somehow miraculously immune to gunfire.

On another occasion when fighting on the frontier, Washington's troops were caught up in a "friendly fire" incident, mistakenly shooting at each other. Washington rode his horse in front of one of the lines of frantic soldiers, using his sword to push their rifles up into the air.[86] Washington estimated that he had closely escaped death four times at this early stage of his military career.

After the frontier fighting, the British turned down Washington's request to be made an officer in the British army, and he retired from the military. He became a businessman, land speculator, and plantation owner.

Two decades later, when he was given command of the Continental Army, Washington's courage remained undaunted by age and station in life. In wartime, Washington continued to express his trust in God on the battlefield. On July 2, 1776, when he took command of the Continental Army, he declared, "The fate of unborn millions will now depend, under God, on the courage and conduct of this army."[87]

One of Washington's officers, Samuel Shaw,[88] wrote home from the warfront on January 7, 1777:

> Our army love our General very much, but yet they have *one thing against him*, which is the little care he takes of himself in any action. His personal bravery, and the desire he has of animating his troops by example, make him fearless of any danger. This, while it makes him appear great, occasions us much uneasiness. But Heaven, who has hitherto been his shield, I hope will still continue to guard so valuable a life.[89]

Was Shaw exaggerating? What sort of risks did General Washington continue to take? Several historians have described Washington leading his men at the Battle of Princeton on January 3, 1777. That event probably influenced Samuel Shaw who wrote his letter of concern four days after the battle. Washington had recently crossed the Delaware on Christmas day and defeated the Hessians in spectacular fashion at Trenton, New Jersey. After the New Year, he again went on the attack, this time at Princeton.

The Americans and the British stumbled upon each other unexpectedly outside Princeton. The Redcoats made a bayonet charge, bloody hand-to-hand combat ensued, and the Americans were on the verge of retreating in panic. Here is historian John Ferling's description of what then took place:

> Seeing what was happening, Washington personally led reinforcements into the fray, staunching the retreat. Sitting high in the saddle on his large gray horse, Washington continued to direct his men from a point no further from the nearest enemy soldier than a pitcher is from a batter on a baseball diamond.[90]

In baseball, the distance between pitcher and batter is about sixty feet. When they want to, pitchers are able to intentionally hit (and sometimes seriously injure) batters with a fastball. The distance is too close even for a trained athlete to duck. Washington was that near to enemy soldiers armed with rifles who could have made history by shooting him dead. As always, he remained unscratched.

Washington Attributed his Military Success to Providence

Washington not only attributed his survival in battle to God, he attributed his military successes to Him as well, including the escape of the Continental Army from almost certain annihilation early in the war in the summer of 1776. The British had defeated the Americans in battles that raged around New York City and the island of Manhattan, finally leaving the main body of Washington's troops trapped in Brooklyn with a wide river between them and their escape. The American troops had to row across the river in the dark of night with their oarlocks muffled to avoid detection. As morning approached, the evacuation was still incomplete.

Then a "strange fog" settled over the area, allowing his entire American army to escape across the river in retreat without losing another man. A little farther south in the same river, the British fleet was forced to remain at anchor in the fog. The prevailing winds also kept them from sailing up the river. Otherwise, the British would have had ships patrolling the area that could have spotted and intercepted the escaping boats as they rowed across the river. Nearby on shore were British cannon that could have been moved into position to blow the small American vessels out of the water. The fog and the adverse winds kept the Redcoats from taking any action against the Americans.

In his book *1776*, historian David McCullough comments on the miraculous escape:

> Incredibly, yet again, circumstances—fate, luck, Providence, the hand of God as would be said so often—intervened.[91]

Some historians make light of Washington's faith in Providence. They say that help from the French rather than God accounted for the American victory. But the French were not there to save the Continental Army on the foggy shores of Brooklyn in 1776. The Continental soldiers were there, the Redcoats were there, and in the opinion of George Washington, God was there as well. A belief in Providence encouraged and supported men like Washington, John and Samuel Adams, Franklin, and Rush. Expressing profound faith in a Guiding Hand, they nonetheless exercised enormous personal discipline and responsibility.

Washington also saw God's hand in his first victory in open confrontation with the whole of the British army. It was June 28, 1778 at Monmouth, New Jersey. Washington had brought his army out of Valley Forge and his advance troops were attacking the rear guard of the British army as it marched toward the safety of the east coast. Abruptly, the American troops closest to the British panicked, broke ranks, and fled smack in Washington's path as he advanced. The British army was in hot pursuit.

Washington stood there in the midst of this turmoil and feared that his army was on the verge of being overrun. It would end the war. Then he looked around and realized "that bountiful Providence which has never failed us in the hour of distress" had in fact stopped him dead in his tracks in a nearly perfect defensive position.[92] He rallied his troops, organized their positions, and defeated the onrushing Redcoats in a bloody battle.

Good fortune or Providence continued to be active in Washington's life. While traveling home by carriage after the Constitutional Convention, Washington and a companion encountered a river that had grown so swollen that it could not be forded. Rather than wait for waters to recede, they crossed on a dangerously old bridge. Rotten planks gave way and one horse plunged fifteen feet into the waters below while the other nearly followed, almost dragging the carriage with it. Fortunately, to lighten the load Washington and his associate had left the carriage to cross the rickety bridge on foot, and they were unharmed.[93] The horses were also saved.

Not long after, in his first inaugural address to the nation on April 30, 1789, Washington reaffirmed his conviction that God had made possible America's victory over Great Britain. He spoke of "tendering homage to the Great Author of every public and private Good" and employed the same "Invisible Hand" image used by Adam Smith to describe the mysterious working of God within society.

FROM WASHINGTON'S FIRST INAUGURAL ADDRESS
APRIL 30, 1789

No people can be bound to acknowledge and adore the Invisible Hand which conducts the affairs of men more than those of the United States. Every step by which they have advanced to the character of an independent nation seems to have been distinguished by some token of providential agency.

Washington "continued to puzzle things out through the eyes of Providence" throughout his lifetime. Shortly before his death in 1799 he wrote about escalating political strife in America: "I have always believed, and trusted, that that Providence which has carried us through a long and painful War with one of the most powerful Nations in Europe" would not allow the recent political bickering to disrupt "the permanent Peace and happiness" of the new nation.[94]

Washington's Sense of Gratitude to God

In his address in 1789 proclaiming Thanksgiving Day, President Washington dedicated the holiday to expressing the nation's gratitude to God for His protection and support. As he had done before, Washington specifically thanked God for His favorable interventions in the War of Independence and for the "peaceful and rational manner" in which the government had been established "for our safety and happiness."

As did many of the Founders, Washington remained concerned about the fate of all humanity. He wanted our nation to be a beacon to others and he concluded his Thanksgiving message by asking God "to grant unto all mankind such a degree of temporal prosperity as he alone knows to be best."

Washington was keenly aware of religious freedom, and in all of his public endorsements of religion and God, he made no specific reference to Christianity. He called upon Americans to base their actions on a belief in a benevolent God. Following Washington's example, to this day our presidents ask for God's help without specifying any one religion.

In chapter 12 we will look further at how George Washington was a source of love—love for his family, fellow soldiers, country, and God. As much as any Founder, and probably more so, George Washington provided us a model for how to guide our lives by freedom, responsibility, gratitude, and love—The Primary Principles:

The Primary Principles
Protect freedom.
Take responsibility at all times.
Express gratitude for every gift and opportunity.
Become a source of love.

From George Washington's Thanksgiving Day Proclamation in 1789

NOW THEREFORE, I do recommend and assign THURSDAY, the TWENTY-SIXTH DAY of NOVEMBER next, to be devoted by the people of these States to the service of that great and glorious Being who is the beneficent author of all the good that was, that is, or that will be; that we may then all unite in rendering unto Him our sincere and humble thanks for His kind care and protection of the people of this country previous to their becoming a nation; for the signal and manifold mercies and the favorable interpositions of His providence in the course and conclusion of the late war; for the great degree of tranquility, union, and plenty which we have since enjoyed;—for the peaceable and rational manner in which we have been enabled to establish Constitutions of government for our safety and happiness, and particularly the national one now lately instituted;—for the civil and religious liberty with which we are blessed, and the means we have of acquiring and diffusing useful knowledge;—and, in general, for all the great and various favors which He has been pleased to confer upon us.

Skeptics About Washington's Faith

Many historians lack faith in the existence of God and even dismiss the importance of faith in other people's lives. They especially don't want to believe that faith in God played a central role in the lives of our great American heroes. As a result, they have argued that Washington was a Deist—someone who believes that the Creator makes no interventions into life on the planet and reveals Himself only through the scientific laws of nature.

Historian Thomas Fleming (2006) decided that his initial impressions were wrong about Washington being a Deist. He concluded that "recent research has revealed a surprising depth to Washington's faith in the divinity."[95] But should Fleming have been surprised? And should he have needed new research? Washington made clear his belief in God in multiple communications from the famous letter to his wife Martha after he took command of the army to his Thanksgiving and his Farewell Addresses.

To his credit, Fleming did change his views, even giving some credence to a much-maligned report and subsequent painting of George Washington praying alone in the snow at Valley Forge.[96] Fleming also cites a deeply moving moment when Washington addressed his troops for the last time after the war:

> George Washington read a brief statement praising the officers and soldiers of the Continental Army for their eight years of service. He also commended "our dear country to the protection of Almighty God." As he said these words, his voice broke and tears streamed down the general's cheeks and he was unable to speak for a full minute. If any further evidence of George Washington's religious faith is needed, it can be found here.[97]

Can we sum up Washington's overall estimate of his role versus God's role in the universe? George Washington had a humble opinion of himself and an exalted opinion of God.

America's Purpose in the World

Washington wanted us to apply the ideal of liberty to every aspect of our lives and even to our relationships with other nations. Applying these principles to foreign affairs in his Farewell Address, he urged the nation to maintain our independence from other countries and to avoid entanglements with them. He encouraged us to show "good faith and justice towards all nations" and to "cultivate peace and harmony with all." Expressing his integrity of values, he explained that "religion and morality" command us to behave in this manner as a nation just as it commanded us to behave this way as individuals. He looked forward to America offering humanity the "novel example of a people always guided by an exalted justice and benevolence."

The same moral principles—liberty, responsibility, gratitude, and love—should guide our lives from the ground up, starting with ourselves. We can live our own lives as ideally as possible and we can be an inspiration to those around us.

A Danger From All Men

John Adams wrote in his personal journal, "There is danger from all men. The only maxim of a free government ought to be to trust no man living with power to endanger the public liberty."[98] Adams thought that all people were driven by ambition and lust for power, so that no one could be trusted with too much power. This is a frightening idea, but it is largely true. Even George Washington proved unwilling during his lifetime to give up the advantages that slavery brought to him and to his family. But Washington's overall life brings us a much more inspiring lesson.

Because of their flaws and inner contradictions, some historians believe that we should not exaggerate the greatness of the Founders. The opposite it true. As a nation we have begun to lose touch with their greatness, their immense contributions to the history of humankind, and their special contributions to each of our lives. We need more, not less, appreciation of the heroic stature of the people who founded our nation. George Washington, John Adams, Benjamin Franklin, Thomas Jefferson, Samuel Adams, Benjamin Rush, and James Madison—these men and dozens of other Founders may have done more good for humanity than any other group of human beings ever to walk the Earth.

John Adams became George Washington's vice-president and was then elected president and served one four-year term. When Jefferson then defeated Adams in a hotly contested and often nasty political campaign, Adams did not try to hold onto his power. Instead he obeyed the Constitution and upheld democracy. He stepped down. In handing over power to the next president, at the time a hated rival, Adams helped America in taking yet another giant step toward the lawful nation that all of us now enjoy.

John Adams and George Washington! Never in the history of the world have there been two consecutive national leaders who brought to their tasks such devotion to liberty and responsibility and such love for their country. We owe a debt of gratitude to them. Humanity's struggle for freedom will forever bear their stamp. They also provide us inspiration in living a life guided by the principles of liberty and responsibility.

Chapter Seven

Benjamin Franklin: The Most Generous Founder

The spirit of liberty in the American colonies allowed people from the most ordinary backgrounds to become giants in history. Benjamin Franklin started life with almost nothing—and if he had been born and lived in England, he never would have been able to make his enormous and indelible mark on history and human existence. There is no way to summarize such an incredibly creative, generous, and responsible life. If he had become nothing else, Ben Franklin would have been the greatest inventor of his century, or its most successful applied scientist, or a famous and enduring author, or one of the world's greatest philanthropists, or one of the greatest heroes of freedom who ever lived.

As a young man, Franklin left home in Boston to find work in a strange city, Philadelphia, where he became a printer and writer. He earned a fortune, wrote a best-selling self-help book that people still read today, helped his community in innumerable ways, developed an astonishing number of useful inventions that improved public health and continue to save lives, became a great scientist, was a leader in the Continental Congress that declared independence from Great Britain, helped to preserve the new nation by acting as its wartime ambassador to France, participated in negotiating the final peace treaty with Great Britain, helped resolve conflicts among the Founders in writing the U.S. Constitution, and in his last years stood up against slavery when others did not dare to stick out their necks.

If he were not so old at the time—he was really a Founding Grandfather—he would have been elected one of the early presidents of the United States.

FRANKLIN'S GENEROSITY

Perhaps because he wrote so cogently about how to make money and how to succeed in business, and perhaps because he became wealthy, Franklin developed an undeserved reputation for being preoccupied with money and material aspirations. Nothing could be further from the truth. He was extraordinarily generous and spent most of his adult life in public service and philanthropy.

HISTORIAN GORDON WOOD FROM *THE AMERICANIZATION OF BENJAMIN FRANKLIN*[99]

He was in fact the most benevolent and philanthropic of the Founders and in some respects the least concerned with the getting of money. Despite achieving fame as a scientist, he never believed that science was as important as public service. Indeed, at the age of forty-two, he retired from business and devoted the remainder of his life to serving his city, his colony, his empire, and then, after independence in 1776, his state and the United States.

THE GENEROUS INVENTOR

Ben Franklin was a most astonishing inventor. Not only was he very curious and inventive, he was motivated to help people.

From bifocals to see close up and at a distance through the same eyeglasses to the odometer that measured the distance a carriage had traveled—almost all of Franklin's inventions aimed at helping people with real-life problems. The goal of making himself useful runs through his entire career, a central theme of his integrity.

Lightning was a very serious problem in colonial times. Lightning bolts not only struck people out in the open, they frequently struck tall buildings, such as large barns and churches with their spires. The strikes could damage buildings, set them afire, and sometimes resulted in deaths.

In his famous experiment, Franklin and his assistant flew a kite attached to a wire during a thunderstorm, and proved that lightning was made of electricity. He then constructed the first lighting rod—a metal pole that catches electricity from the lightning strike and directs it harmlessly through a wire into the ground. Within a few years, lighting rods were protecting buildings throughout America and Europe—and they continue to do so more than two hundred years later.

Ben Franklin knew that wood-burning fireplaces in homes were inefficient—that most of the heat went up the chimney. Fireplaces also belched smoke and sickened the air inside the house. So he invented the Franklin stove. Made of iron, the stove stood within the room itself, radiating as much heat as possible, and the smoke was vented through a pipe out of the building.

It was already possible in those days to patent inventions—to keep possession of the idea or design, and to make money from selling it. Ben Franklin could have become even wealthier by patenting his inventions. Instead, he offered them as gifts to humankind.

FROM *THE AUTOBIOGRAPHY OF BENJAMIN FRANKLIN*

As we enjoy great advantages from the invention of others, we should be glad of an opportunity to serve others by any invention of ours, and this we should do freely and generously.

Ben Franklin even invented new institutions to serve the public. He developed the first fire department in the world and the first insurance company in America. He inspired the creation of the University of Pennsylvania and the U. S. Postal System. In his elder years, he contributed to the writing of the Constitution of the United States of America.

THE SCIENTIST

Ben Franklin's study of electricity was far more extensive than flying a kite or building a lightning rod. He developed many basic concepts that we continue to use today in understanding electricity, such as insulation and conductors. He invented the first battery for storing electricity. Probably because he was more practical than theoretical in his focus, his contributions to science have not been fully appreciated.

Franklin was very interested in weather and was probably the first meteorologist—a scientist who studies weather. By exchanging letters with a friend several hundred miles away, Franklin showed that storms did not necessarily come from the direction of their winds. He was able to trace the route of a storm that came up from the south, even though its winds were blowing from a different direction. He also discovered the Gulf Stream—the flow of ocean water that moves from south to north along the American coast, helping to keep it warm. Franklin also found that fruits and vegetables, when eaten by sailors on long voyages, would prevent scurvy. Without identifying it, Franklin had discovered the effects of Vitamin C.

The Author

If he'd done nothing else, Ben Franklin's autobiography would be among the all-time bestsellers. It was the first autobiography of a "common man" and also the first self-help book. Oh, yes, he may also have been America's first political cartoonist. Remember the cartoon in which the colonies were drawn like a snake cut into separate parts? Ben Franklin created and published that cartoon with the comment, "Join, or die."

The Economist

Franklin also wrote about economics—the study of how wealth is produced. Earlier I mentioned that Franklin met Adam Smith, the author of *The Wealth of Nations,* when he was living in England. Smith's famous book utilizes some of Franklin's work about the effects of America's vast space on its population and wealth.

The Most All-Around American

Ben Franklin was not only a great Founder—he may have been the most accomplished all-around man who ever lived. In school nowadays there is an excessive emphasis on being an "all-around" young student. Most people don't get ahead by being good at many things. Success is about finding what you love and can do well, and courageously persisting at it. At the same time, it's about discovering your way of contributing to others, to society, and to the world. But if we wanted to give out a "Best

All-Around Founder Award," Ben Franklin would win it hands down.

With all his incredible accomplishments, Franklin's most astonishing quality may be his sense of virtue or ethics, and especially his generosity. He believed in doing good things for others and made innumerable contributions to his community, to his nation, and to humankind.

Franklin's good humor and wisdom helped to resolve conflicts among the sometimes-feuding representatives from the colonies. There is a story that when John Hancock signed his name to the Declaration of Independence with that grand flourish, he said, "There must be no pulling in different ways. We must all hang together." Franklin is said to have replied humorously, "Yes, we must indeed, all hang together or more assuredly we shall all hang separately."[100] In his generosity, Franklin was willing to risk his life for his ideals and for the future of humanity—and even to joke about it. At the time he took this risk, he was the most famous and respected American in the world, so he had a lot to lose.

Finally Refusing to Compromise on Slavery

In his later years, Franklin took yet another risk on behalf of freedom. For more than a decade, the Founders decided to remain silent on the subject of slavery in their debates and formal pronouncements. They wanted the Southern slave states to sign the Declaration of Independence and to participate in the Revolution. Still later the Founders agreed to ignore the crime of slavery so that the same southern states would ratify the Constitution and join the United States of America. The Founders continued their unholy silence about slavery when the U. S. Congress began meeting for the first time.

Early in his career Franklin seemed little concerned about slavery and at one point he may have even owned some house slaves. But as he grew older and wiser, he took a deeper look at this moral abomination. He became president of an abolitionist society and dedicated himself to opposing slavery. It may be hard to imagine this, but it was considered "radical" and "dangerous" in America to be absolutely against slavery. With Benjamin Rush as another important exception, most leaders wanted to continue compromising.

Franklin became outraged by speeches in Congress that tried to use Christianity and the Bible to justify slavery. Shortly before his death, in his subtle and amusing way, he pointed out that the Southern gentleman's words were strangely similar to those of an Algerian pirate who had tried to use Islam and the Koran to justify the enslavement of Christians.[101]

Franklin made up the pirate story, but it was founded in truth. For generations, Islamic pirates had used the Koran to justify robbing the ships of "infidel" Europeans and seizing the passengers for ransom.

A Lesson from the Barbary Pirates

When Jefferson and Franklin were diplomats to France they were appalled by how the Europeans allowed the Muslim pirates to extort fortunes by capturing and ransoming European ships and passengers. Writing in 1996, five years before the attack on the Twin Towers in New York City and before Islamic terrorism had become so notorious in the public's mind, historian Joseph Ellis described how John Adams and Jefferson had written to Congress to alert America to what Ellis called "terrorism."

Historian Joseph Ellis from *American Sphinx* [102]

In a joint message to their superiors in Congress, Adams and Jefferson describe the audacity of these terrorist attacks, pirates leaping onto defenseless ships with daggers clenched in their teeth. They had asked the ambassador from Tripoli, Adams and Jefferson explained, on what grounds these outrageous acts of unbridled savagery could be justified: "The Ambassador answered us that it was founded on the Laws of the Prophet, that it was written in their Koran, that all nations who should not have acknowledged their authority were sinners, that it was their right and duty to make war upon them where they could be found, and to make slaves of all they could take Prisoners."

Both Adams and Jefferson were against negotiating with the Islamic terrorists; but, lacking a navy, Adams the realist recommended paying them off for the time being. Adams prophetically explained, "We ought not to fight them at all unless we determine to fight them forever."

Later when he was president, Jefferson refused pirate demands for an annual payment of blood money from the U. S. government. The pasha of Tripoli then declared war on the United States. Jefferson sent the U.S. Navy to the Mediterranean to fight the pirates in what became America's first international police action. Naval battles with the Islamic raiders continued throughout most of Jefferson's presidency. These military actions are immortalized by the phrase "to the shores of Tripoli" in the United States Marine Corps hymn.

The first struggles with Islamic terrorists took place more than two hundred years ago. Some mistaken Americans believe that the Islamic terrorists are largely motivated by real grievances against us. Americans need to know that Islamic terrorists were attacking U.S. shipping long before this nation had become involved in any way in their affairs and that they justified their terrorism on the basis of the Koran—exactly as they do today.

Ben Franklin and Democracy

Like most colonists, Ben Franklin did not start out being a rebel. He was a successful businessman who, early in his career, wanted to help the colonists maintain their relationship with King George and the British Empire. He lived and worked in England, where he represented the financial interests of several colonies, and felt closely identified with many influential British people. But as the American colonies became more determined to seek independence, Franklin had a change of heart. He returned home to support the revolution in every way that he could. Franklin was a man who, with experience, grew in his understanding of politics and human rights.

Some Founders were aristocratic in their thinking—they saw themselves as special because they belonged to an educated, landed, or wealthy elite. These Founders were leery of democracy. They especially feared mob psychology and the potential excesses of a democratic majority. With Franklin's enormous financial success, his worldwide fame, and his good relationships with British nobility—he easily could have come to think of himself as an aristocrat. Instead, he never lost sight of his humble origins.

Among the Founders, Franklin was one of the stauncher advocates for democracy. He wanted to establish a society in which every single person would have the opportunity to improve his or her life, and he pushed the Constitutional Convention in the direction of more democratic processes than desired by most of the Founders who remained cautious about giving too much power to the people. For example, he wanted a single house of representatives that would not be constrained by a senate.

Unlike an aristocrat, Franklin never took for granted his good fortune in life. Although he emphasized how hard and responsibly he had worked, he never stopped thanking God for the blessings in his life. Regularly thanking God for our good fortune helps us to maintain perspective.

Belief in Providence

The flawed humanity of the men who founded our nation is nowhere more obvious than in the jealousy they sometimes displayed toward one another. Coming from a Puritanical perspective, John Adams wrote disparagingly of Franklin while in Paris in 1777-1778. He saw Franklin as materialistic, intellectually shallow, irreligious, wallowing in the adoration of the French, and frivolous in his social activities.[103] He complained that Franklin never told anyone that he believed in God. Franklin at this time was an elderly gentleman in his seventies and he would soon beg Congress to retire him from foreign duty, so that he could return home.[104] Before departing he would help to negotiate a treaty of alliance with France. In 1782 he would participate in negotiating the peace treaty with Great Britain, and then he would return home again to participate in writing the Constitution, and then in opposing slavery—all shortly before he died in 1790.

The attack by John Adams on Franklin on religious grounds is disappointing. Given Franklin's contributions to humanity, he would have been a great and generous man even if he lacked religiosity or a belief in God. Nonetheless, Franklin made clear that he believed in God, in the hand of God in our lives, and even in an afterlife. Like many of the Founders, Ben Franklin was interested in discovering the most important religious ideas, the best principles offered by religion. In *The Autobiography of Benjamin Franklin,* he lists his own beliefs, derived from what he saw as the best of religion:

> That there is one God, who made all things.
> That he governs the world by his providence.
> That he ought to be worshiped by adoration, prayer, and thanksgiving.
> But that the most acceptable service of God is doing good to man.
> That the soul is immortal.
> And that God will certainly reward virtue and punish vice either here or hereafter.

Historian Walter Isaacson observed that Franklin reaffirmed this "basic creed" one month before he died.[105]

John Adams and George Washington seemed to share most of Franklin's beliefs, in particular gratitude to God for our blessings and the importance of living life for the benefit of all people. George Washington, for example, could have said these words that were written by Ben Franklin:[106] "If it had not been for the justice of our cause and the consequent interposition of Providence, in which we had faith, we must have been ruined."

Franklin added that if he had not believed in God, then America's success in the War of Independence would have made a believer out of him. Only God's intervention could have given America its victory against the mighty British Empire.

Exactly as Franklin saw God's intervention in the War of Independence, he also saw that same Invisible Hand in his own life. On the opening page of his *Autobiography,* he thanked God for his happiness and for any future happiness that he might be permitted to enjoy.

From *The Autobiography of Benjamin Franklin*

And now I speak of thanking God, I desire with all humility to acknowledge that I owe the mentioned happiness of my past life to His kind providence, which lead me to the means I used and gave them success. My belief of this induces me to hope, though I must not presume, that the same goodness will still be exercised toward me, in continuing that happiness, or enabling me to bear a fatal reverse, which I may experience as others have done: the complexion of my future fortune being known to Him only in whose power it is to bless to us even our afflictions.

For Franklin, John and Samuel Adams, and Washington, belief in divine intervention did not relieve them of responsibility for taking charge of their own lives. If anything, it increased their sense of duty. After all, if their projects in this world were worthy of God's attention and intervention, then surely these same projects were worthy of their own best efforts as well. For these Founders, life was a joint venture with God working toward the fulfillment of the same values and ideals for oneself and for all other human beings. They saw themselves working in partnership with God for the benefit of all. None of them would have tried to face life's challenges without seeking God's support any more than they would have gone hiking in freezing cold without clothing.

Responsibility for Our Everyday Lives

As already described, Benjamin Franklin repeatedly declared that the best way to serve God was by doing good for people. He expressed gratitude to God for treating him so well and tried to show gratitude by giving back to God's other children.

Historian Walter Isaacson from *Benjamin Franklin: An American Life*[107]

His morality was built on a sincere belief in leading a virtuous life, serving the country he loved, and hoping to achieve salvation through good works. That led him to make the link between private virtue and civic virtue, and to suspect, based on the meager evidence he could muster about God's will, that these earthly virtues were linked to heavenly ones as well. As he put it in the motto for the library he founded, "To pour forth benefits for the common good is divine."

Ben Franklin's List of Virtues

When he was sixty-five, Benjamin Franklin started to write his autobiography. Like so much else that he did, it was a first. There was no precedent for a self-made man to tell the story of his life. As previously stated, it was also the first self-help book. He was living in Great Britain at the time and had not as yet returned to America to participate in the revolutionary changes.

In several famous passages in *The Autobiography of Benjamin Franklin,* Franklin wrote about how, in his early twenties, he decided to work toward "moral perfection." He wanted to rid himself of all faults. But he found that as soon as he managed to get one fault under control, another popped up. So he tried to focus his attention on a limited number of virtues—thirteen to be exact: Temperance, silence (speak only when it's helpful to others), order, resolution (keeping your word), frugality, industry, sincerity, justice, moderation, cleanliness, tranquility, chastity, and humor.

Most of Franklin's virtues remind us to be aware of our impact on others and to make our effects as beneficial as possible. The exercise of many of these virtues is guaranteed to improve our relationships with family, friends, and everyone else whom we touch. Other principles affirm responsibility—to do only what's right, to do your duty, and to always follow through on your promises to yourself and to others. He urges us to give up resentments and minor irritations, and to see the bigger picture.

Franklin concludes his virtues with humility and urges us to "imitate" two of the greatest sources of truth in the Western world: Socrates and Jesus. Remember our earlier discussion about where the colonists obtained their ideas? The ancient Greek named Socrates is one of the fathers of Western philosophy and Jesus, of course, is the source of Christianity. Both Socrates and Jesus died for their beliefs. Together, Socrates and Jesus exemplify the Enlightenment that inspired the colonists—the remarkable coming together of philosophy and religion that urged us to live according to the principles of liberty, responsibility, gratitude, and love.

ENJOYING LIFE

Despite his call for seriousness and hard work in his autobiography, Franklin retired young and went on to greatly enjoy life. During the War of Independence, when he went to Paris to represent the United States, Franklin basked in the adoration of the French. There are many stories of how much time he devoted to entertainment and an active social life. As we've seen, the more somber and puritanical John Adams resented this. Franklin might have retorted that his job as ambassador required winning over the French people to like him and to enjoy his company. The French certainly loved Ben Franklin—all to the benefit of the United States.

In honor of Benjamin Franklin's later years, I would add this to his list of virtues: Good Humor: Have a lot of fun; enjoy yourself and other people. Whether he would endorse this, I cannot be sure; but I am certain that he would embrace each of The Primary Principles:

THE PRIMARY PRINCIPLES
Protect freedom.
Take responsibility at all times.
Express gratitude for every gift and opportunity.
Become a source of love.

Throughout his senior decades of life, Franklin devoted himself to protecting and extending freedom, sometimes at grave risk to his reputation, wealth, and life. His devotion to America's political future took precedence over his many other interests, abilities, and contributions, including science, writing, and business. In his publications and through his actions, Franklin repeatedly demonstrated the importance of taking full responsibility for oneself at all times and in every way. Responsibility was his mantra. Like all the Founders we will meet, he felt and expressed gratitude to God for the good in his life and for guiding America to victory in the War of Independence. He has been described as lacking emotional depth in his personal relationships;[108] but his life demonstrated the profoundest love for liberty, humanity, country, and God through his infinite variety of good deeds and good works.

Chapter Eight

The U. S. Constitution—Our Ship of Freedom

Late one night when I was in the middle of writing this book, I was fast asleep when I began making sounds in my sleep as if trying to talk. According to my wife Ginger, she gave me a nudge and asked, "What's going on?"

Still asleep, I replied to her, "I'm loading the ship."

"Where's it going?" she asked me.

In one of those sleepy, almost ghostly voices, I replied with certainty, "Freedom."

What needs to be loaded onto the Ship of Freedom?

The first thing our ship needs is ideas. Huge ideas that give weight and strength to the keel beneath ship, keeping the craft stable and erect, and straight on its course. Ideas about freedom and responsibility. Ideas about inalienable human rights, including life, liberty, property, and the pursuit of happiness. Ideas about democracy. Ideas about the free enterprise system that enables people to generate wealth and to lift up everyone's standard of living.

The ship must have a place of honor for the Declaration of Independence, the Constitution of the United States, and The Bill of Rights, where the crew and the officers can daily renew their appreciation of the marvelous principles that guide the Ship of Freedom. Everyone on board needs to celebrate and to love these great documents.

The crew—that's all of us!

The ship needs an educated crew, citizens who know the history of America, citizens who understand the importance of the big ideas that stabilize and guide the ship, citizens who think of the Founders as their political family of origin, citizens who understand that with freedom comes responsibility. These citizens must know that voting is a duty of every citizen, but that no one can vote your rights away. Democracy is not an end itself; democracy is the best method for protecting individual human rights, yours and mine, and every other person here on Earth. They must know that progress is about increasing human rights everywhere in the world.

The Ship of Freedom needs reliable officers and a captain chosen by its citizen crew. These leaders do not have to be the brightest, the most imaginative, or the most exciting among us. Our leaders should not be chosen to make things better by themselves or on their own, or by virtue of their personal intelligence or charisma. They must see themselves as stewards or caretakers of the great ideas that give the people energy. They must be devoted to protecting freedom and encouraging responsibility. Their job is to make sure that the ship's sails are filled with the spirit of freedom and self-reliance that permeates our souls. They must keep the ship pointed in the right direction—toward spreading freedom to every soul on Earth.

The ship also needs weapons—heavy guns that it can stick out its gun ports to protect itself. Some people believe that "being good" is enough to make us safe. But in the entire history of the world, being a worthy person or a worthy nation has never made anyone safe—and it never will. That's because human nature contains more than love of freedom and devotion to responsibility. Human nature has darker corners. Fear lurks in one terrifying corner and helplessness in another. Because human nature is imperfect, some people can always be whipped up into hating and envying freedom and its wonderful rewards.

The weapons must be kept in reserve as last resorts. They must never be fired except in self-defense. The ship's greatest strength comes from its ideas. The Ship of Freedom must communicate its ideas to other ships and to other nations all over the world. It needs to proudly declare, "Here we are, we're America, the Ship of Freedom. We are hope! We will support you in your efforts to fulfill your human rights through democracy, freedom and responsibility."

We are blessed to live on the Ship of Freedom. Enjoy the great opportunities, and help to keep the ship afloat and steered in the right direction.

A Coalition of Independent States

The U.S. Constitution was not written until seven years after the British were defeated at Yorktown. After the War of Independence was won, the thirteen independent states were afraid of joining together to create another government that might someday become as threatening as King George and Parliament. They knew that governments are always dangerous—always quick to take more power from the people. So they lived under a weak national government based on the Articles of Confederation. Called the United States of America, they were united mostly in name only.

Under the Articles of Confederation the states remained largely self-governing. The new federal government was so weak that it could not adequately manage the frontier, defend the colonies, make treaties with foreign nations, and carry out other important activities. The War of Independence had cost a great deal of money, and without a stronger central government, there was no way to pay off the debts.

MAKING A MORE PERFECT UNION

More than ten years after the Declaration of Independence, the Founders again met to debate the kind of government that they wanted and needed. Initially they planned to modify the Articles of Confederation; but under the leadership of James Madison they began to rethink the whole idea of government.

Many of the Founders who fought for America's independence were still actively involved in creating the new Constitution. George Washington was chosen to lead the new Constitutional Congress, lending great authority to its deliberations. Ben Franklin was eighty-one years old, tired and frail, but he attended all but one of the conference days.[109] Although Franklin had many reservations about it, he urged the delegates to accept the final compromise document. Jefferson was away in Paris as the U. S. Ambassador to France but had written to James Madison that he generally supported a constitution. John Adams was away in London as ambassador to Great Britain and he too wrote home in favor of the constitution. All of these Founders continued to be active in forming the new government after the war; and of course after returning to American soil, Adams would be elected our second president and Jefferson our third. In 1809, Madison would follow Jefferson to become the fourth President of the United States.

In the same way that the Founders saw the War of Independence as a struggle for universal human rights, they saw the creation of the Constitution as an inspirational model for self-government throughout the world. In advocating ratification of the Constitution, John Jay declared that the Constitution would demonstrate for the first time that human beings were capable of "establishing good government from reflection and choice" rather than by leaving it to "accident and force." Not succeeding in the creation of an American government, he warned, would be to "the general misfortune of humankind."[110]

Conflicting Values

The Framers of the Constitution tried to weigh and to balance ideas that were sometimes in conflict with each other. Each new state—they were no longer colonies—wanted to keep its own independence and character but most felt the need to strengthen the federal government. The smaller states like Rhode Island and Delaware were afraid of being dominated and overwhelmed by larger states like Massachusetts, New York, and Virginia. The more populous states didn't think that the smaller ones should have an equal say under the new government. How could large states and small states get together under one strong government?

The Founders were also concerned about maintaining individual rights. A strong federal government could trample on individual rights, including life, liberty, property, and the pursuit of happiness.

The Founders were sympathetic to democracy—to the right of the people to make their own laws and choose their own leaders. But they also feared democracy—the capacity of the majority to suppress minority religions, ideas, or interests. They didn't want democracy to threaten individual human rights. In short, they didn't want the many to bully the few. They also feared that unbridled democracy could lead to anarchy, and that would be replaced by a more oppressive form of government.

In addition to these conflicts, slavery remained a dreadful and seemingly insurmountable source of conflict. The economies of Virginia, North and South Carolina, Georgia, and portions of Maryland remained deeply dependent on slavery. Many white people in those states could not imagine maintaining their way of life without slavery. These states would not join a national government without an agreement to preserve the existence of slavery. But slavery offended every American ideal, including liberty, human rights, and democracy. A nation that drew heavily on the Judeo-Christian ideal of "Do unto others as you would have others do unto you" was hard pressed to justify the enslavement of hundreds of thousands of people.

Praying at the Constitutional Convention

Benjamin Franklin proposed that a daily prayer might help to break the deadlocks among the delegates. In his prayer, Franklin compared the convention representatives to the builders of the Tower of Babel. In the biblical story, men defiant of God decide that they can build a tower to heaven; but God causes chaos among them by forcing them to speak so many different languages that they cannot work together to complete their task.

Benjamin Franklin's Prayer to the Constitutional Convention in 1787[111]

The longer I live, the more convincing proofs I see of this truth, that God governs in the affairs of men. And if a sparrow cannot fall to the ground without his notice, is it probable that an empire can rise without his aid? We have been assured, Sir, in the sacred writings, that "except the Lord build the house, they labor in vain that build it." I firmly believe this; and I also believe that, without his concurring aid, we shall succeed in this political building no better than the builders of Babel.

Franklin made his point that the framers of the Constitution would have to speak to each other and to compromise in the interest of their larger task, with faith in the Creator's unseen hand to guide their deliberations.

Franklin himself had to compromise. He argued against having a legislature with two separate bodies, a House and a

Senate, warning that like a two-headed snake it could be torn apart trying to go in different directions. It's said that he brought along a pickled two-headed snake for a "show and tell" to illustrate his point. And Franklin was growing to loathe slavery, but he again compromised by temporarily putting aside the issue. The presence of greatly admired men like Washington and Franklin enabled others to join in finding mutually agreeable or at least tolerable compromises.

Forming a Union

The Founders began to build a government from scratch—one that would bring together the ideas of freedom, individual rights, and democracy. Where they used to think of themselves as Virginians or New Yorkers, they now began thinking of themselves as Americans. And their political ideas were becoming bolder. Instead of believing that governments have rights, they increasingly emphasized that individual people have rights. The new federal government would draw its power from all the people. This was embodied in the Preamble or introduction to the new Constitution, which begins,"We the People of the United States..."

The Preamble to the Constitution of the United States of America

We the People of the United States, in Order to form a more perfect Union, establish Justice, insure domestic Tranquility, provide for the common defense, promote the general Welfare, and secure the Blessings of Liberty to ourselves and our Posterity, do ordain and establish this Constitution of the United States of America.

The Framers of the Constitution envisioned a government in which the voters had a voice in choosing their president and representatives—but not so much democracy that the majority could shout down the minority. Having "the people" create their own government was a good idea; but the Founders did not want the people to become like a mob that acts irrationally and threatens individual rights. They also feared the thirst for power in individuals. Instead of Utopia, they planned a government with built-in checks and balances—rules that would restrain human passions such as greed and lust for power. They would rely on enforcing "the rules of the game" rather than on any idealistic notion of trusting human beings to be good.[112] So the Founders created a Republic in which the people could vote for their leaders and representatives; but the power of the government would be forever limited or restrained by a series of "checks and balances" to protect the rights of the individual states and especially individual citizens.

The new Constitution of the United States of America provided for three separate branches of government to share power with each other—the Congress, the President, and the Supreme Court. These are the legislative, executive, and judicial branches of the government, and they were intended to provide checks on each other's power. All this was determined after great thoughtfulness and strenuous argument that continued throughout the colonies during the time leading up to final ratification by the states.

Very wisely, the Framers decided to create two separate legislative bodies to make the nation's laws. In the Senate every state would have an equal number of votes. That gave the smaller states an equal voice and made them feel more secure. In the second part of the legislature, the House of Representatives, each state was represented according to the size of its population. That gave the larger states more of a voice, and also moved the country closer to a democracy where every citizen has an equal vote in choosing his or her representatives.

The problem of slavery was once again mostly ignored. It was like a cancer that no one dared to look at, let alone operate on. The slave states were allowed to count a portion of their slaves as citizens in order to give them a larger census and hence more voting power; but of course the slaves would not be able to vote.

Under the Constitution, the importation of slaves into the United States could not be banned for twenty years, until 1808, at which time Congress did pass legislation prohibiting it. But banning the slave trade actually made existing slaves even more valuable to their owners. Meanwhile, slavery itself was not limited by the Constitution and it continued to thrive in the Land of the Free until the Civil War.

B. J. Lossing from

Signers of the Declaration of Independence[113]

The final adoption of the Federal Constitution and the organization of the present government of the United States under it, formed the climax—the crowning act of the drama of which the Declaration of Independence was the opening scene.

Opposition to the Constitution

There was a great deal of opposition to the new Constitution and its ratification by the states was hard fought. Vigorous debates took place throughout the individual state conventions. Many citizens feared that the Constitution made the federal government much too powerful and that the presidency would degenerate into a monarchy. Although this worst-case scenario have not yet materialized, the power of the national government has indeed bloated beyond the worst fears of the Founders.

Those in favor of a strong executive branch claimed that a more powerful president would enable the nation to respond more vigorously and rapidly to crises such as war. George Mason of Virginia disagreed. He found the strength of the nation was not in its leaders but in its "invincible" people:

> This invincible Principle is to be found in the Love, the Affection [and] the Attachment of the Citizens to their laws, to their Freedom, and to their Country.[114]

At the present time in our history when many citizens have become enamored with a charismatic leader who promises to save us from disaster, this warning is especially appropriate. Our nation must be built on the strength of a free people, and not on the strength of a leader full of promises. Although George Washington was worshipped by many of his contemporaries, he always acted with restraint, placed the law of the land above his own ambitions, and viewed himself as an instrument of freedom and a servant of the Constitution rather than a savior.

Washington Becomes the First President of the United States

The Constitution was approved by the individual states in 1788 and the next year George Washington was elected the first President of the United States of America. The Constitution was a document, words on paper. George Washington made it real by adhering to its principles.

We have seen that Washington could have made himself President-for-Life or even King George of America. But our first president had dedicated his life to the values expressed in the Declaration of Independence and the Constitution, and later the Bill of Rights. It's worth repeating that when George Washington peacefully handed over power to the next elected President of the United States, John Adams, the Founders continued to keep their word. They also kept their faith. They remained true to the principles of liberty and personal independence upon which they had founded this nation. Now it is up to all of us, and to future generations, to carry on the sacred duty of standing up for America—for a nation that protects and promotes freedom and responsibility.

Chapter Nine

The Bill of Rights— Our Shield of Freedom

Our daughter Aly was always a free spirit, and sometimes a defiant one as well. In that regard, she was like almost any child destined to become a remarkable and admirable adult. When she was a little girl, my wife Ginger and I frequently took her for walks around the neighborhood. She was about five years old on this particular day when she complained loudly, "I don't want to go for a walk."

There's a part inside each of us that says, "I want to do what I want to do!" We never quite outgrow it.

On this walk, Aly began to act tired and bored, and she complained about wanting to go home. She started lollygagging instead of walking beside us. This went on for a few blocks until we reached a little park with slides and swings, places to crawl around and climb, and an expanse of lawn. All of a sudden, Aly knew exactly what she wanted to do, and as if magically transformed she ran like the wind with her arms outstretched like the wings of a bird. That wonderful feeling of bursting full of energy—that is the feeling of freedom. A person who feels free feels full of energy.

Aly is married now and recently we had a visit from her, her husband Chris, and our grandson Cole. If you are reading this,

Cole, I can tell you that from the time you were little, you had a mind of your own. Even as a fifteen-month-old your independent spirit was obvious. You entered a room and took command of it, toddling from one interesting object or challenge to another, touching and handling one thing after another, climbing onto or over one obstacle after another. You enjoyed playing with me while you were exploring, but your intent was clear—pursuing whatever caught your eye as if you owned the world. The drive to explore the world—to express your own personal preferences and your freedom—was built into you.

You were just learning to say words, but you already acted as if you had rights, in particular the right to explore every aspect of anything that drew your attention, no exceptions. You would have taken a stand and made a fight of it if I tried to prevent you from pursuing whatever caught your interest, including a fragile vase or treasured art object. You would not put up with being forcibly restrained from doing or trying anything. You brushed off even the slightest attempt to hold your arm back or to guide your hand away from anything against your wishes. But fortunately you were still young enough to be easily distracted by a playful grandfather, and you lit me up with your giggly smiles.

The Founders of this nation knew that freedom is the engine that powers people to accomplish amazing things. They knew that freedom was making colonial America bustle with productive activities.

Born to Own Property

Just as they are born with an innate impulse to be free, all children are born with a drive to take possession of stuff for their own use and enjoyment. Raw human nature in a two-year-old screams, "Mine!" But it takes more maturity to realize that other people have exactly the same right to the exclusive use of their own property.

As children grow older, they find that their rights sometimes clash with the rights of other children and family members. They may want to hog another child's toy, but the other child or an adult might disagree. Learning that our own rights depend on respecting each person's rights is a big part of growing up and living a good life—and it's also part of understanding what makes our country so great. Our Founders believed that freedom and property were complementary rights upon which to build a good life and a strong nation.

Author Dinesh D'Souza[115]

The modern idea of freedom...is rooted in a respect for the individual. It means the right to express our opinion, the right to choose a career, the right to buy and sell property, the right to travel where we want, the right to our own personal space, and the right to live our own life. In return, we are responsible only to respect the rights of others.

Rights Versus Privileges

Children often think that they have a right to something; but their parents will view it as a privilege that they may or may not decide to grant. Rights belong to us; privileges are granted to us.

Before the United States of America came into existence, most adults in the world were treated like children. They had few rights. Instead, they were granted privileges.

In Great Britain, changes were already taking place during colonial times, and the king's subjects also had some rights—but most of these were not firmly established. Great Britain did not have a Bill of Rights and therefore neither did the colonies.

Because of the Founders we live in a country that will recognize our rights when we grow old enough to take responsibility for ourselves. We are not forced to remain like children, asking or begging for privileges from the government. We are citizens with the right to life, liberty, property and the pursuit of happiness—to do the best that we can do with our own property and lives. At least, that was the hope of the Founders—a hope that every generation must protect and even expand to include all citizens.

Children Have a Different Kind of Rights

Because children are relatively helpless and dependent, everyone now agrees that they have special rights. Staying up late or watching TV may be a privilege. Eating candy may be a privilege. But as a child in America, and in many other countries, you have a legal right not to be abused or abandoned. You also have the right to food, shelter, and education during your childhood. If your parents fail to provide these necessities, then government authorities are supposed to step in to assure that your basic needs are met.

Increasingly, the needs of children are being redefined as rights, but there is disagreement about how far this expansion of rights should be taken and how these needs should be met—by a combination of the free enterprise system and charity or government and bureaucracy. Health care lies at the center of this dispute. Right now in America poor children are given access to doctors and hospitals through a variety of government programs. Should all children, rich and poor, be provided healthcare by government the way they are provided public education through high school? Questions like this may be decided in the near future. Although the goals are often well intentioned, we must remember that the more the government provides these services, the less adequate the services will be, and the more that freedom and responsibility will be eroded. More people will be pushed from independence into dependence.

Children have special rights because they are incapable of taking responsibility for themselves. As a child you are dependent on others for your basic needs. When the family cannot provide for those needs, then the government intervenes. But in recent times the distinction between adults and children has become clouded. Many people think that adults should have the same or similar rights as children, for example, to be guaranteed food, a home, and an education, or to be rescued from financial mistakes or mishaps. Especially when adults are having difficulties, as in tough economic times, the government increasingly treats them as if they cannot take responsibility for their basic needs or, on an institutional or societal scale, for their mistakes in business or finance. Treating adults as if they have the rights of children is taking America in a direction that the Founders never favored—an issue that will be discussed in later chapters.

Need for a Bill of Rights

Remember how the Founders wanted to protect citizens from being abused by their own government? Even after the Constitution of the United States was approved and George Washington became the first president, the Framers and the American people continued to worry and to argue among themselves about how best to protect individual human rights. They had fought, and some had died, in the name of these rights. Now the Constitution created a government that was so strong that it might threaten individual rights, such as freedom of religion and freedom of expression. The new government might try to control the press or to jail people who disagreed with it. It might threaten the rights of people to own and to control their own property.

The Founders decided to add a Bill of Rights to the Constitution. Some wanted to hold up completion of the Constitution and to include the Bill of Rights within it; but others were eager to get the new government on its feet. The Bill of Rights would become the first ten amendments to the already approved and working Constitution.

In the whole world, there was nothing like a Bill of Rights—a document confirming that your individual rights come ahead of everything else, including any tendency your government may have to abuse you.

Although the U. S. Bill of Rights was adopted in 1789, its evolution began much earlier—thousands of years earlier. Remember that chapter 4 asked, "Who made up these ideas about liberty, human rights and democracy?"

The concept of a list of human rights was traced back to the Ten Commandments in the Old Testament, which in effect protects us from false witnesses and from those who would desire our property. It also protects of us from being cheated, lied to, and stolen from.

American Precursors to the Bill of Rights

On November 20, 1772 a Boston Town Meeting approved a statement of "Rights of the Colonists" which was drafted primarily by Samuel Adams. Although a relatively poor man who displayed little or no acquisitiveness, Adams's three basic rights included property: "First, a Right to Life; Secondly to Liberty; thirdly to Property."

According to historian Ira Stoll, this document "provided a framework for the Declaration of Independence and, in some ways, the First Amendment to the Constitution that eventually followed."[116]

Now let's pick up the story a few weeks before the signing of the Declaration of Independence when Founder George Mason drafted a Bill of Rights for Virginia. On June 12, 1776, Mason's proposal was modified and then the Virginia Convention approved its sixteen articles. Notice the sentiment of Article 1 from which Jefferson would borrow his famous declaration of "unalienable rights." The Viginia version differs mainly in its emphasis on the right to acquire and possess property.

Virginia Bill of Rights, Articles 1 and 16
June 12, 1776

That all men are by nature equally free and independent, and have certain inherent rights, of which, when they enter into a state of society, they cannot, by any compact, deprive or divest their posterity; namely, the enjoyment of life and liberty, with the means of acquiring and possessing property, and pursuing and obtaining happiness and safety.

That religion, or the duty which we owe to our CREATOR, and the manner of discharging it, can be directed only by reason and conviction, not by force or violence; and therefore all men are equally entitled to the free exercise of religion, according to the dictates of conscience; and that it is the mutual duty of all to practice Christian forbearance, love, and charity, towards each other.

Virginia slaveholders feared the original wording, which did not contain the phrase "when they enter into a state of society." Such an uncompromising confirmation of human rights without any qualification could legally abolish slavery[117] or incite the slaves to rebellion.[118] Against Mason's wishes, the Convention added the new phrase, indicating that people do not have "inherent rights" until "they enter into a state of society."

Slaves, these Virginians argued, had not yet entered such a state. Of course, these same slave owners were using every violent means at hand to prevent them from entering into American society.

Jefferson would leave out the right to property from the Declaration of Independence, perhaps to avoid a conflict over the concept that slaves were considered by many to be a legitimate form of property.[119]

Thus, America continued to evade its most dreadful issue—the moral and political abomination of owning black people as property. Meanwhile, ownership of "property" remained a central theme throughout the revolutionary era. When inspiring his troops, General Washington exhorted them to fight for "Life, Liberty, Property and our Country."[120]

The Massachusetts Declaration of Rights

Four years later in 1780, Massachusetts approved its own Declaration of Rights as a part of its new state constitution—now the oldest functioning written constitution in the world.[121] Written by John Adams, it also empasizes property rights. Article I reads:

> All men are born free and equal, and have certain natural, essential, and unalienable rights; among which may

> be reckoned the right of enjoying and defending their lives and liberties; that of acquiring, possessing, and protecting property; in fine [briefly], that of seeking and obtaining their safety and happiness.

Notice the close connection between this political statement and real life experiences of acquiring and protecting property, and seeking and obtaining safety and happiness. People have a right to defend themselves and their liberties. People have a right to acquire, own, and protect their property. People have a right to enjoy their lives and to seek happiness. That's you and I, and everyone else. We have the right to pursue our own happiness as long as we respect the equal rights of others to do the same.

Adams went a step further in the Declaration of Rights, instructing the government and its officials to encourage and to instill in the people "the principles of humanity and general benevolence, public and private charity, industry and frugality, honesty and punctuality in their dealings; sincerity, good humor, and all social affections, and generous sentiments..."

This sweeping moral mandate, written by John Adams, was accepted without modification by the state convention.[122] One imagines that Ben Franklin, with his emphasis on virtues, would have agreed.

The U.S. Bill of Rights

Under the leadership of James Madison, the Framers proposed more than ten amendments to the Constitution. The states ratified ten of them and on December 15, 1791 they became the Bill of Rights. This occurred during George Washington's first term as president.

A Bill of Rights! With the exception of some individual American states, nothing like this had ever existed in the world—a statement about the limitations of government and the rights of all citizens. To this day, the Bill of Rights remains the bedrock upon which our freedoms are built. People continue to cite the Bill of Rights when they argue about the extent of our rights and how to apply them to our everyday lives in America.

The First Amendment is only one sentence long but its meanings and interpretations could fill a large library.

The First Amendment to the Constitution of the United States

Congress shall make no law respecting an establishment of religion or prohibiting the free exercise thereof; or abridging the freedom of speech, or of the press, or the right of the people peaceably to assemble, and to petition the Government for a redress of grievances.

Put into simple terms, these are the freedoms that the First Amendment guarantees to Americans:

Freedom of speech
Freedom of religion
Freedom of the press
Freedom to gather peacefully
Freedom to protest to the government about its actions

Never before in history had a government been based on respect for the individual rights of its citizens.

Here, again in simple terms, are some of the additional rights summarized in the Bill of Rights:

The right to be free from government abuses or intrusions into our lives, homes, and property.
The right to be free from government threats to our lives, liberty, and property such as illegal government searches, takeovers, or controls.
The right to own guns.
The right to a speedy public trial and to confront our accusers.
The right to trial by jury.
The right to be free of cruel and unusual punishments.

The Framers built a protective wall around every American citizen. Think of it as one of those invisible electric fences that keep dogs from leaving their yards. Every time the dog tries to cross the electrical barrier, it gets shocked by its own collar and jumps back. Every time the government tries to cross the line to abuse an American citizen, the electric fence called the Bill of Rights is meant to shock the daylights out of the government intruder.

The Founders did not want the government to claim, "Your rights are limited to those that are listed in the Bill of Rights. You don't have any rights that aren't listed." So the Bill of Rights states that we keep any rights that haven't as yet been mentioned or specifically transferred to the government. Human rights are God-given, natural, and inalienable; they belong to us as much as our mind or spirit.

The Bill of Rights is far more important than any one of the individual rights that it protects. It is more important than all of those rights put together. The Bill of Rights reminds us that individual rights are the foundation of our government and our way of life as Americans.

Remember that the Ten Commandments told us what rights belong to God and what rights belong to human beings.

The Bill of Rights told us what rights belong to the government and what rights remain with the people. The Bill of Rights grew directly from the Declaration of Independence with its inspiring statement:

> We hold these truths to be self-evident, that all men are created equal, that they are endowed by their Creator with certain Unalienable Rights, that among these, are Life, Liberty, and the pursuit of Happiness – That, to secure these rights, Governments are instituted among Men, deriving their just Powers from the consent of the governed.

Our basic human rights are the foundation of this nation and the building blocks of our individual lives.

In a more personal way, the Bill of Rights is about individual responsibility and respect for others. Because we have the rights to life, liberty, property, and the pursuit of happiness, we also have the responsibility to exercise them—to be responsible toward ourselves and toward others.

There is nothing in the Bill of Rights about relying on the government to give us our rights; we already possess them and must be vigilant against the government trying to take them away. There is nothing in the Bill of Rights about the government giving us houses or property; it forbids the government from taking away or misusing our houses and property—at least, not without "due process" or established legal procedure.

The Bill of Rights tells us that we must respect the right of every American to take responsibility for his or her own life, liberty, property, and happiness. American citizens must respect each other's rights; this is at the heart of being an American.

America isn't perfect and it never will be. You and I are not perfect, and we never will be. But we live in a nation built on the idea of basic human rights, starting with the freedom to take responsibility for our own lives. To the degree that our government protects these rights, we have the opportunity to build the kinds of lives that we desire while we respect the right of everyone else to do the same thing.

The Declaration of Independence, the Constitution of the United States of America, and the Bill of Rights are much more than historical documents hidden behind glass in the U. S. Archives. They continue to influence every aspect of our lives. They not only provide protection for our personal rights, they say something universal and eternal to us about human rights and human dignity. They represent the blood, sweat, and tears of the Founders and millions of other Americans who fought for and helped to create this nation.

Chapter Ten

Keeping the Wow! in America

Happiness comes from the responsible exercise of freedom. That's the personal lesson provided by Founders like John and Abigail Adams, George and Martha Washington, and Benjamin Franklin.

Other than by taking charge of our lives and making the most of the freedom that's available to us, there is no way to become genuinely happy. When responsible and free people experience love for their families, friends, community, and God, they become as fully happy as possible here on this planet.

So happiness comes from the responsible exercise of freedom—but that fact of life has never stopped people from trying to get happy by every imaginable shortcut. People try to get happy by hitting the lottery. They try to get happy by overeating, taking drugs, and drinking alcohol. They try to get happy by making money illegally. They try to get happy by getting the government to take care of them at the expense of others.

Genuine, lasting happiness comes from doing what's right. That means living by principles and high ideals—the same principles and high ideals that the Founders put into the conduct of their lives and into the Declaration of Independence, the Constitution of the United States, and the Bill of Rights.

CHANGING IDEAS ABOUT RESPONSIBILITY AND FREEDOM

Not everyone agrees with what I'm saying. Nowadays, the government intrudes into every aspect of society from businesses that are failing to people who don't save enough money to take care of themselves. Remember my painful discovery: well-meaning government workers will even clip the "weeds" from in front of your house—not knowing they are ripping up your prized butterfly bushes.

Founders like George Washington, John Adams, Benjamin Franklin, Samuel Adams, James Madison, and Benjamin Rush never imagined relying on government for kindness, generosity, and charity. They knew that citizens had to be free to take responsibility for their own lives, and they expected them to turn to private charity for help when necessary. When people are free to take care of themselves, they will also be kind and generous to other people.

Most of the Founders gravely distrusted government. They worried about creating one of their own, knowing that governments always were an endless source of mischief. It was obvious to them from history, and from living under the British Empire, that every government enlarged its own power, stole from its own people, and made unnecessary wars against other peoples.

The Founders thought that government was a necessary evil—something very dangerous and potentially evil, but seemingly indispensable. A federal government was needed to provide people with a safe community in which to live and work. In the Constitution of the United States, that was called "ensuring the domestic tranquility."

The new national government was not supposed to take care of everybody's needs. The Founders of our nation believed that freedom and opportunity were the best way to provide for the great majority of people and that private charity could respond to those in need.

Many Americans have forgotten, or never knew, what has made America the land of opportunity. Remember, I started out by explaining that the United States of America is so wonderful because the ideas of the Founders are the same ideas you need to build a good life for yourself. The most basic idea of all is your freedom to take responsibility for yourself.

Of course, no one expects a child to be responsible all the time. That's part of learning as we grow up. But life will not be generous to us as adults the way it may have been when we were children. Reality is demanding. When you are an adult, you will botch up your life every single time you fail to take responsibility for yourself. There are few if any exceptions to this rule. When you are an adult, life will bite you back every single time you fail to take charge of yourself and your actions. Conversely, your life will go best whenever you determine to do what's right and to take responsibility for your actions in every situation at all times.

The Real Mayflower Story

Many people know something about the Pilgrims: How they fled Europe to come to America on the Mayflower seeking freedom from religious persecution; how they celebrated the first Thanksgiving; and how eventually they succeeded in making a thriving colony in Plymouth, Massachusetts. Unfortunately, some historians have misled us into believing that the Pilgrims survived largely because the Native Americans taught them how to grow and gather food. The Indians did help the Pilgrims through the first winter. But by the second and third winters, many of the settlers were starving to death. If the Pilgrims had not drastically changed their attitudes toward freedom and responsibility, they would not have survived.

Before they stepped off the boat onto the shores of the new continent, the Pilgrims signed a famous agreement called the

Mayflower Compact in which they promised to work obediently for the common good. This is a very different idea from the right to life, liberty, property, and the pursuit of happiness. For the Pilgrims, the starting point was the community rather than the individual. You worked for the community ahead of yourself and your family. As a result, private property was not sacred and inviolable, as it would become to the Founders.

In keeping with this focus on the common good, the Pilgrims decided that every family should contribute the food that it grew to a community storehouse for everyone to share. They viewed this as the religiously correct way for people to live and they believed that it would help everyone to survive. Instead of private property, they emphasized communal property.

It didn't work out well, especially after newcomers with less religious zeal and community spirit arrived at Plymouth the second year. The vulnerable aspects of human nature took over and some people worked much harder than others at cultivating food crops. Others were lazy or irresponsible, and yet expected to get fed. When the unfairness became obvious, normally hardworking people stopped working as hard as they could. Nearly half of the Pilgrims starved to death in the first few winters in America.

In desperation, the leader of the Pilgrims, Governor William Bradford, had a dramatic change of heart. Turning to the Bible in a new light, he found this verse: "If any man would not work, neither should he eat."[123]

Each Pilgrim family was given a private plot of land to cultivate and each was allowed to keep all the food that it could grow. Previously hardworking people once again became industrious. Slackers who initially refused to work quickly learned that the Pilgrims meant business—that each person had to work in order to eat. According to Bradford, "Any general want or suffering hath not been among them since this day."[124] Nobody starved to death anymore.

Nathaniel Philbrick from *Mayflower*[125]

The fall of 1623 marked the end of Plymouth's debilitating food shortages. For the last two planting seasons, the Pilgrims had grown crops communally—the approach first used in Jamestown and other English settlements. But as the disastrous harvest of the previous fall had shown, something drastic needed to be done to increase the annual yield.

In April, Bradford had decided that each household should be assigned its own plot to cultivate, with the understanding that each family kept whatever it grew. The change in attitude was stunning. Families now worked much harder than they had ever worked before....The Pilgrims had stumbled on the power of capitalism. Although the fortunes of the colony still teetered precariously in the years ahead, the inhabitants never again starved.

Unfortunately, most historians ignore these events or give them only passing mention. That's one of the reasons I have written this book—to remember the truth about what makes American society work. It begins with people pursuing their own interests and taking care of themselves and their families; and when those efforts have established prosperity, these same people become more willing and able to share. Also, as Adam Smith explained, in the process of pursuing their own interests they increase the wealth of society.

FORCING PEOPLE TO SHARE

The idea of government forcing people to share most of what they create or produce has never completely died out. Based on the philosophy of communism as developed by Karl Marx, coercing citizens to share has been tried under dictatorships in the Soviet Union, the Peoples Republic of China, North Korea, and Cuba. Everywhere and every time it has resulted in the collapse of progress, in grinding poverty, and often in mass starvation. Even on a small scale, for example in communities called communes inside the United States over the past few centuries, these experiments in sharing have rarely lasted any length of time.

While he was fighting the Revolutionary War, George Washington understood the futility of trying to bend human nature to unrealistic expectations of self-sacrifice. In writing to Congress about the war effort, he emphasized the importance of paying the soldiers what they had been promised. Patriotism was a powerful motive—especially early in the war when emotions ran high—but personal interests also required consideration, especially when asking soldiers to devote years of their lives to the Cause. Washington warned,"Few men are capable of making a continual sacrifice ... to the common good." As if taking a lesson from the failed Pilgrim experiment, he added,"...the experience of every age and nation has proved it." He further explained, "We must take the passions of Men as Nature has given them, and those principles as a guide which are the general rule of Action."[126]

If future philosophers and politicians had been as realistic and wise as Washington, the tragic experiments in communism would never have taken place. If today's politicians took heed of Washington's observations, they would not be so eager to dismantle our capitalistic system in favor of a more socialistic redistribution of the wealth.

The key to modern progress? Individual human beings set free to work as hard and imaginatively as they can and wish. The free enterprise system, or capitalism, is the engine of progress that has provided an abundance of food and material goods throughout the western world, including Europe and North America.

The Future of Our Grandchildren

Almost everyone agrees that the United States has become so huge and complicated that people cannot always obtain the help they need from charity. So it becomes a matter of balance.

The government needs to provide some help to people who are having difficulty taking care of themselves and their families; but it must be careful not to encourage helplessness and dependence, and it must be wary of taking too much money away from those people who generate wealth. By the standards of our Founders, the balance has gone out of whack and America is in danger of becoming a nation like any other nation, where people depend too heavily upon others to run their lives.

When individuals become accustomed to the idea that the government will take care of them, many stop taking care of themselves. We all know children who seem to get whatever they want from their parents by complaining or throwing a temper tantrum. That's going on right now in our nation. A lot of people are complaining and pressuring the government to give them what they want. From powerful corporations and labor unions to individual people—a mighty clamor has arisen from those who want "their piece" of the government pie. The trouble is, it's not really the government's pie to give away.

America's children and grandchildren are in danger of growing up in a world where the government functions mainly to take care of people. If that transformation goes much further,

America's children and grandchildren will be pressured to go along with being dependents of the state for much of what they need or desire. Instead, I hope future generations will remain determined to take care of themselves and their families, and anyone else they care about. I hope they will be so strong—so responsible—that they will make the most of life even when the government makes a bigger and bigger mess of things. I hope they will lend their support to the eternal struggle to promote the ideals of liberty and responsibility, while they live by The Primary Principles:

The Primary Principles

Protect freedom.

Take responsibility at all times.

Express gratitude for your gifts and opportunities.

Become a source of love.

Remember that the Founders believed in basic human rights. The most basic right is individual freedom. Freedom provides the opportunity to take responsibility for your own life. The Founders knew that people perform on a much higher level when they are free to take care of themselves and to pursue their own self-chosen interests and passions. They understood that free and responsible people are happier, more prosperous, and more generous and charitable. They could see it in the bustling lives of people living and working in the colonies from north to south, and on the western frontier.

Don't let America fizzle out. Let's keep the "Wow!" in being an American—the marvelous opportunity of living in a nation where we are free to choose our own paths and to work toward our own goals.

Chapter Eleven

When "Dependence" Meets "Independence"

Imagine a world made up of two different people with very different and conflicting ideas about themselves and their basic rights. One is named Dependence. Dependence doesn't think he can earn enough money to pay for what he needs and wants, such as food, shelter, medical care, education, and retirement. He wants the government to provide these things for him. The other person is Independence. He wants the government to protect his freedom to take care of himself.

Meet "Dependence"

Dependence not only wants government help in fulfilling his own desires, he also feels sympathy for other less successful people and wants to see life made easier for them. His focus is not on individual freedom and responsibility; his focus is on getting the government to guarantee the fulfillment of his basic needs as he defines them.

Dependence feels inadequate to meet the challenges of life and believes that many other people are at least as much if not more inadequate. Life sounds too risky for him to rely on himself. He thinks it's unfair for him and his family to suffer, and he wants his government to make up for this unfairness by helping him out. On top of this, he has been taught that the government can be trusted to guarantee him a good job, food, shelter, healthcare, education, and retirement income. Dependence feels entitled to these benefits of the good life; it's his due, something he deserves to have. Nowadays he thinks it's his right.

Meet "Independence"

The person named Independence has very different ideas that might even offend and distress Dependence. Independence is determined to make enough money to pay for what he needs, such as food, shelter, and medical care. He plans to earn enough for extras as well, for things he and his loved ones enjoy. And he's made up his mind to take care of his children, including their education, and to make sure he's not a burden on anyone in his old age. He is up to the challenge, knows it will require hard work, and feels energized to make the effort. He believes that he has the right to take responsibility for himself and to keep most of his earnings for himself and his family.

Independence is willing to give to charity and he often does. Sometimes he gives to family or community; sometimes he may give to a formal charity like the Red Cross or Salvation Army. Frequently he volunteers at church, the fire department or other public service institutions. But he resents being forced to give "charity" through taxes that are collected and redistributed by the government—with most of it being wasted or gobbled up by the government and its interest groups. He does not want to share his hard-earned money with people like Dependence who feel entitled to be taken care of and who don't work as hard or behave as responsibly as he does.

Although he believes in generosity and charity, he does not believe that people have an inalienable right to be taken care of.

John Adams to His Son Thomas about Entering Government Service or Politics[127]

A young man should weigh his plans well. Integrity should be preserved in all events, as essential to his happiness, through every stage of his existence. His first maxim then should be to place his honor out of reach of all men. In order to do this he must make it a rule never to become dependent on public employment for subsistence. Let him have a trade, a profession, a farm, a shop, something where he can honestly live, and then he may engage in public affairs, if invited, upon independent principles. My advice to my children is to maintain an independent character.

What If They Met Each Other?

Remember that we're imagining a world in which there are only two people. Dependence is one and Independence is the other. In the world of politics, there are millions of people like Dependence and millions of others like Independence, and many who are a combination of both. But what if they were two separate people—what would it be like when they met? They probably would not get along very well.

Independence would probably resent Dependence for using the government to take away so much of his money. And Dependence would probably resent Independence for "being rich," even though Independence is sharing his money with him by paying taxes and giving to charities.

Where Does the Money Come From?

People like Dependence who receive help from the government often imagine that the money "comes from the government," but it's really other people's money. The government doesn't earn money; it takes it away from other people like Independence and redistributes it. If the government borrows money long-term, then it must be taken away from future generations—forcing children born in the future to shoulder the debts of earlier generations.

If the government simply prints money without taking or borrowing it from taxpayers, then the money will drastically lose value over time. Innumerable governments throughout history have turned themselves into money printing machines and each time this has caused their money to drop in value or become worthless. During the War of Independence, money printed by the Continental Congress lost so much value that people spoke of things without value as being "not worth a Continental." During the Civil War, people who accepted money printed by the southern Confederacy ended up losing everything. Before becoming collector's items, Confederate bills were used for wallpaper. People who get stuck with worthless U.S. dollars in the future will pay a dreadful price for the government's current irresponsibility in printing and borrowing far too much money.

The person I've named Dependence doesn't like to face the fact that somebody else had to earn any money that's transferred to him by the government. Or he thinks that it comes from taxing "rich people" who don't deserve it or who won't miss it. Today, America's leaders have encouraged class conflict in which Independence has become fair game for Dependence to prey upon. In terms of who pays income tax, more people still pay income tax than not; but at the rate that "soak the rich" is being encouraged, soon less than half the nation's adults will be paying income taxes.

In recent times, the government has advocated placing even heavier taxes on "the top 2% of the richest people." In a democracy, where everyone gets to vote, this obviously has a lot of potential appeal to the remaining 98% of people. But this is exactly what the Founders feared about democracy—that the many would gang up on the few.

If there were only two people—one being taxed and one receiving benefits from the taxes—then it would be much easier to see that money is simply being forcibly transferred from Independence to Dependence. Imagine if Dependence had to stick out his hand—or his gun—and demand money directly from Independence. That sounds like panhandling or robbery. Well, the basic underlying principle doesn't change when there are three or four people involved, or even when there are millions of people taking money away from other people. Those who take money can only get it from those who make money and are forced to give it up.

Of course federal and state governments need money to provide military and police protection, infrastructure and some essential services, including help for the poor; everyone nowadays realizes and accepts this. What people don't fully grasp is that even the most useful government services or benefits require taking money from Independence to pay Dependence. Often this involves taking money from the most hardworking people and giving it to the least hardworking.

Remember how the American colonists rebelled against paying taxes to the King of England? It drove them to want independence. In order for the government to give money to one person, it must tax another person. There's no way around this simple fact. And it's even worse in the way it actually works. Because the government wastes so much money, it must seize much more money from Independence than it will ever redistribute to Dependence. For every bite of food the government gives away, it is likely to gorge itself and its supporters while letting much of it go to waste.

Remember how the Pilgrims began starving to death when responsible people were forced to share the food they grew with the whole community? Without the incentive of keeping their own food, hardworking families stopped working so hard, and slackers didn't work enough to keep themselves from starving. But when these same hardworking families became free to work for their own benefit, they ended up growing much more food. Even more telling, when no one got free food on demand, they found ways to work for their food or to rely on charity. No one starved.

Nowadays, Independence is being forced to give away more and more of his money. If it hasn't happened already, eventually he's going to stop working so hard. And he won't have enough money to run the businesses that employ other people. When that happens, there won't be any money left for Dependence no matter how loud he screams and shouts.

Soaking the Rich—Not Such a Good Deal for the Poor

Income tax doesn't tell the whole story. Although it's true that the overwhelming amount of income tax in the United States is paid by a few percent of relatively wealthy people, the poor pay much more in taxes than they realize, for example, in sales taxes, gasoline taxes, and various fees from auto licenses to bridge tolls.

Also, taxes on the rich filter down and end up being paid by the poor in the form of costlier goods and lower wages. Higher taxes also tend to discourage individuals and businesses for investing their money and creating new jobs, and that harms everyone in the economy, especially the poor.

Then there is the cheapening of the money through inflation. This, too, hits the middle class and working people the hardest when they have to buy essentials like food, clothing, and housing at higher costs. Unlike the rich, most people have fewer opportunities to protect or to increase their income as inflation drives up the costs of their essentials.

Never forget that the free market, with all its human flaws, is largely responsible for the enormous increase in human wealth and all other forms of progress over the past few centuries. Most of the poor in America today live better than the wealthy before the advent of economic freedom. As others have pointed out, the unemployed in this nation often live better than the employed in many other nations. That's one reason why Mexico's poor try so hard to get into this country and to sign up for various benefits.

The Odd Thing About Responsibility and Gratitude

There is an odd thing about responsibility. You might think that people who work harder than most would want to take most of the credit for themselves; but in my experience, the opposite is true. The harder people work, the more thankful they feel for whatever they are "given" by life in the way of opportunity and success. People like Independence almost always express gratitude for everything they receive.

We have documented that three of the most responsible men who ever lived—George Washington, John Adams, and Benjamin Franklin—throughout their lives expressed gratitude to God for what they had achieved and for the success of their country. Benjamin Rush and Samuel Adams also freely thanked God for blessing them and their nation. So did James Madison.

George Washington exemplified gratitude. He was a self-educated, self-made man who worked hard in his youth to apply moral principles to his life. He courageously faced death, continued to work incredibly hard in every aspect of his life, stayed true to the Cause through all kinds of dangers and disappointments—and throughout, remained grateful to Providence. As we've seen, his Thanksgiving Proclamation called upon the nation to dedicate a day in gratitude to God for His blessing on our nation and on us as individuals. Washington often said that his own capacities as a general were in no way sufficient to have led to the victory of the Americans over the British. He felt humbled by his successful escapes and his victories on the battlefield, and he ascribed them to God. Repeatedly, he expressed gratitude and encouraged others to express it as well.

Now consider this: People like Dependence who do not like to take responsibility for themselves almost never give thanks for what they receive. People who wrangle favors out of other people, who get handouts, and who live off others almost always feel entitled rather than grateful. Without lifting a hand to get what they want, they nonetheless feel as if they deserve everything they get—and more. Indeed, they typically feel resentful toward the people who ultimately provide for them.

Why do people who work harder than other people usually end up feeling grateful for what they get? Why do people who don't work as hard often end up feeling resentful instead of grateful for whatever they receive through the generosity of others?

I believe there is a core in every one of us that knows we should take responsibility and do what's right. When we act in accordance with our true or best nature, we feel good about ourselves. We know that hard work doesn't guarantee success, but we work hard because it's right, because it's consistent with our human nature, because it increases the chances of success, because we like the feeling of self-esteem that comes with making an effort, and because we want to contribute to our loved ones and society. Then we are grateful for the good result whenever it comes.

So why don't slackers feel even more grateful when they are given things without making an effort? Perhaps on some level, irresponsible people know that they are offending their own true or best nature. They sense that they are taking advantage of others. They have sunk into an unethical condition in which they cannot feel comfortable with themselves. They feel ashamed of themselves and they resent responsible people whose lives remind them about their own spiritually sorry condition.

People like Dependence actually resent The Primary Principles for reminding them about the values of freedom, responsibility, gratitude, and love.

Is There a Right to be Taken Care Of?

When the Founders invented this country, they were entirely on the side of the person I'm calling Independence. They hardly knew anyone named Dependence, and they didn't offer him anything in the Declaration of Independence, the Constitution, or the Bill of Rights. The Founders wanted to provide Americans the opportunity to be self-reliant and to seek their own happiness. Beyond guaranteeing people their God-given rights to life, liberty, property, and the pursuit of happiness, they had no desire for the government to become a giant charity. They feared that government might be dominated by legions of dependent voters and interest groups demanding more and more handouts. In fact, they were terrified of this happening, and created checks and balances in part to prevent this dreaded outcome.

The Constitution of the United States and the Bill of Rights say nothing about a right to be taken care of. There's nothing about the right to have your life made easier for you. The Bill of Rights aims at protecting our basic human capacity to live responsibly in a free nation.

Ben Franklin, John Adams, and George Washington knew that hard work increased one's opportunities without guaranteeing success, and they would have been appalled at changing the rules of life that were derived from God and human nature. Franklin and Rush were particularly interested in providing charity for the poor and as much education as possible for everyone. Mostly they tried to implement this through private charity and by improving a limited number of public institutions, such as prisons, hospitals, and schools. They never imagined that taking care of people would become a major government activity, let alone *the* major government activity. If the government continues to spend as much as it now does on entitlements such as Social Security, Medicare, and Medicaid, there will soon be no money left for anything else, including "national defense, energy, education, the whole works."[128]

Concern for Others

Today we know that complex modern societies need government services and a safety net. One of the most important and expensive in America is Social Security. People pay into Social Security while they are working and the government is supposed to return the money in payments during their retirement years. Another is Medicare, which pays most of the medical bills of older people. Yet another is Medicaid, which provides healthcare and other services to the poor. There are many additional government programs to help relatively poor families and especially disadvantaged children. Other programs provide for the disabled.

These government services provide increased security or a "safety net" for those who need help. But there's a negative trade off to these seemingly benevolent efforts. These same programs tend to create larger numbers of dependent people with reduced motivation to take responsibility for themselves and their families.

Beyond that, Social Security, Medicare and similar entitlements are not genuine insurance programs. The payouts exceed the total amount that's paid in by the recipients, and so the payouts are collected from general revenues—from all the taxpayers. As a result, there are no built-in limits to how extravagant these programs can become.

It is like a mathematical formula. Provide government aid to anyone, from big businesses to individual citizens, and increasing numbers will line up asking for money, forfeiting responsibility in favor of dependence on the government. Provide yet more money, and yet more businesses and citizens will line up. And so on... In economics this unintended consequence has been poignantly named the "moral hazard."

The question is no longer, "Should the government provide a safety net?" The question is, "How much safety net and at what cost to the taxpayer?" Another question is, "How much chronic dependence do these programs cause?" And yet another is, "At what point, are we no longer a free society with a free enterprise system?"

Meanwhile, most of the existing programs including Social Security and Medicare have become so bloated and mismanaged that they will become overwhelmingly burdensome to coming generations. They are going broke and within a generation they may break the nation's economy.

Early in my career, when I was a full-time psychiatrist in the U. S. Public Health Service at the National Institute of Mental Health (NIMH), I learned that government agencies frantically spend all their remaining money as the year comes to a close. If they are left with extra money, they will not be congratulated for saving money. Instead, they will find it harder to demand bigger budgets the following year. Obtaining more money each year is the primary drive of all government agencies.

On the one hand, people will always line up for any handout from the government. On the other hand, the government always tries to get more money to hand out. The pressure continually moves toward larger government—and everywhere in the world, governments have been getting larger and larger, taking and wasting more and more of the people's money.

As government agencies increase in size—and they always try to expand—a larger segment of the population learns to become dependent on the government. Whatever good it may do, this government support for individuals and corporations will also undermine responsibility and self-reliance, and breed inefficiency, waste, and dependence. Any government bailout carries with it this moral hazard—the risk of discouraging productivity and creativity, while encouraging irresponsibility and failure.

When taking care of the poor and less fortunate, we must never lose sight of where the resources come from. Individuals exercising their freedom in a responsible fashion create these resources. The more the government offers security and dependence, the more it must reduce the freedom of its citizens by making more rules and regulations, and by seizing more and more individual wealth through taxation.

The government's main purpose should be the protection of individual freedom. To the degree that the government protects liberty, there will be resources to share with those who are in need.

Bread and Circuses

Two thousand years ago, the Roman emperors gave "bread and circuses" to the poor to keep them from rebelling and to distract them from demanding real opportunities in their lives. They gave the poor crumbs of food off their overflowing dinner tables rather than giving them a chance to earn a living. They put on violent circuses to entertain them, rather than allowing them to participate energetically in the productive life of Rome.

Eventually the poor began to think that they were entitled to bread and circuses. It was their right. Once this happened—once they demanded security instead of freedom and responsibility—they were lost. They would remain dependent on whatever the emperor handed out to them.

The bread and circus approach increasingly dominates American politics as politicians give away more and more money in return for votes. Instead of encouraging people to become more independent, these politicians have encouraged them to scream and shout for immediate help. Many of these beneficiaries could become more able and more responsible, but the politicians encourage them to remain stuck in their feelings of helplessness.

It is a terrible thing to teach people to scream and shout for help when they are capable of learning to take care of themselves. Earlier, I compared this to "spoiling the child." Many politicians spoil the people who vote for them, encouraging them to ruin their lives, ultimately placing an increased burden on hard working Americans. The politicians do this to buy votes. To keep getting the votes, they must keep their supporters screaming and shouting for help.

Powerful corporations and labor unions, and varied lobbying groups from banks to unions and environmentalists have much more clout than ordinary folks. They have the power to make outright demands and they receive billions and even trillions of dollars while the suffering of more innocent and less powerful individuals goes unrelieved.

The American dream is in danger of fading over the horizon like a sun setting for the last time. America, the beacon of freedom, can never mainly be about rescuing or taking care of people, corporations, labor unions, or any other institutions of society. America became the most marvelous nation in the history of the world by providing extraordinary opportunity to its citizens while offering hope to people all over the world that they, too, might someday win the freedom to take responsibility for themselves.

Yes, some government help will always be necessary for individual citizens who become unable to take care of themselves, especially when that happens through no fault of their own. But rescue and help cannot become the big idea behind government—or the wonderment will be taken out of America.

In my area of the country in upstate New York there is a little town named Locke. It sits in a valley carved out millions of years ago by the glaciers. One day a big truck lost its brakes on the road that leads downhill to Locke. The truck slammed into a beautiful historic bank building on the corner of the crossroad in the middle of Locke, utterly destroying it. The more modern replacement structure was tawdry at best.

This really happened. And on a much larger scale, it is happening to all of America. Like a runaway truck, our government has lost its brakes. This rogue truck may be unstoppable and it may demolish the symbolic bank of America—the great energy of this free people.

Around the world, modern democracies are becoming more focused on security than on freedom, responsibility, and independence. This was not the vision of America that the Founders had in mind. They created a government that unleashed the creative energies of individuals. This—and not security—has made our citizens the most productive on Earth and our country the most powerful in the world. The freedom to take responsibility has made us the shining light to other people and nations.

Progress through Applying Human Rights

Suppose that Dependence was a victim of racism, sexism or some other social condition that prevented him from enjoying the rights guaranteed to all Americans?

The Founders knew that some Americans were disadvantaged—that the law or prejudice prevented them from exercising their basic human rights. Adams, Washington, and Jefferson thought that slavery was evil and, despite their compromises, they knew it had to end someday. From early in his life, Benjamin Rush was an abolitionist, and Ben Franklin became one later in life. Eventually, the founding principles of America could no longer be withheld from its most oppressed minority. After bloody conflict, slavery was abolished. Then the freedom movement led by Martin Luther King, Jr. abolished legalized segregation and continued to expand the inclusion of African-Americans into society as equals.

Some Founders realized that women were disadvantaged. Remember that Abigail Adams tweaked her husband John about how he and his male colleagues failed to include women or their rights in their deliberations? Once again, these men compromised with human rights, while their principles about human rights sowed the seeds for the eventual political equality of women.

By establishing the concept of universal human rights, the Founders set up the mechanism for remedying injustices. Every injustice today requires that same remedy—providing and expanding freedom for all people to exercise their abilities in a responsible fashion.

What America Gives to the Rest of the World

Americans make a potentially tragic mistake when we think that sharing our wealth with other nations is the best kind of help we have to offer. Yes, in emergencies such as natural catastrophes, we should donate a portion of our wealth and we are among the most generous nations in the world when it comes to doing that. But in the long run, the money and resources we give as gifts are easily stolen, diverted, wasted, or simply used up. Aid in the form of money, products, and food can never do as much good as helping a country to take care of itself through establishing political freedom and free enterprise.

Donations of money are easily diverted into hands of powerful politicians who use the cash to support themselves and the corrupt government that has already failed its people. Donations of goods and food can actually discourage local businesses and farms from meeting the future needs of the people. While the charity is pouring in, providing some immediate relief to people, local businesses and farms have less opportunity to sell their products. When the charitable donations run out, the businesses and farms in the meantime have downsized or gone under.

Human nature is no different in the United States, Russia, China, India, or Iraq. The Declaration of Independence and the Bill of Rights are universal; they apply to everyone everywhere on Earth. The whole world needs exactly what has made America so great—freedom and responsibility, the opportunity for the individual to pursue life, liberty, property, and happiness. America can best serve humankind by growing stronger as an example to the world—the beacon of freedom and responsibility that our Founders expected us to become.

Chapter Twelve

Become a Source of Love

It was a few months before my grandson Cole's first birthday, and I took time off to travel from New York to Florida to visit with him, my daughter Aly, and her husband Chris. I was recuperating from an injury in an auto accident and, at my age, it can take longer to heal. I was tired and I had a lot on my mind as well. I won't bore you with the details, but basically I was feeling a bit overwhelmed and maybe a little old.

Cole, there's no way you will remember this, so I want to record it here for you to read in the future and also to use the story to illustrate for everyone what I mean by love. Grandma Ginger could not make the trip, but we both decided that a visit to see you and your mom and dad might perk me up.

"Perk me up" is hardly sufficient to describe how good it was to see you and your parents. Soon after I arrived, you and I spent time together playing, and then you napped a while on my chest. I fell asleep too. And then we both woke up refreshed and feeling really good about each other. You were touching my face and we were smiling at each other. At that magic moment, your grandpa Roy took a photograph that shows us looking at each other with smiles that burst out with happiness from inside ourselves. Me especially. I'm holding you and grinning into your smiling face, and I look as happy as a man can be. I didn't know that I could glow like that.

You know how sometimes a small child can get a silly grin on his or her face. Other times a child can laugh at something funny. This was different. Looking at you was lighting up my soul and the light illuminated my face. That's what I mean by real deep love. It lights up your soul and spills over the people around you.

Real deep love tells you what really matters. It brings you back to life when you're losing energy or feeling downhearted. Even under the most difficult circumstances, it can bring moments of happiness. Real deep love makes you joyful about someone or something beyond yourself. It signals what matters—and you matter a great deal to me.

In my life, your Grandma Ginger is the most real, deep love that I have ever known. It's been that way for 25 years and it just keeps on getting realer and deeper. I hope you—and everyone reading this book—will find this for yourself someday, so that you will feel grateful for every moment you share with your special person. I also hope you will be able to feel this kind of happiness about your family, your work, nature, and God.

People Are Made of Each Other's Love

Cole, without your mother and father's love, you would not have become such a remarkable and able child. And your mother and father would not have become such good parents without the love and support of their parents. Do you see how love flows from generation to generation? And when it fails to flow, people suffer and must struggle harder to put love into their lives.

Untold numbers of people—starting with your mom and dad, their parents and grandparents—contributed to that wonderful moment when you and I awoke and smiled at each other. Your mom and dad love me and welcomed me into their home, or I wouldn't have been so happy and relaxed. Your grandpa Roy was enjoying both of us or he never could have snapped such a perfect photograph of that smiling moment. Your grandma Ginger loves us and encouraged me to make the trip to visit with you even though she had to stay home. Most important, her love for me has enabled me to experience real deep love.

Even Ginger's mom, your Great Grandmother Jean, who was far away in Indiana was there in spirit. I feel her presence right now as I'm writing this, and I know how happy it makes her when her children and grandchildren enjoy each other. When we experience love, we feel connected to everyone we love and to everything good in the universe.

And God was there as He always is when people love one another. That's why real love lights up our souls; God is the ultimate source of the love within us. When you and I were feeling so much love for each other, God was giving us a glimpse of what life is ultimately all about.

Cole, it's extraordinary but true: You are already a source of love. Love beams out of you. You shine it on the people around you. It's like a miracle. Think of the sun. It warms and lights the Earth and provides energy for everything that grows. Our love is like sunshine to each other. We warm and light up each other, and renew each other's energy. It's every person's private miracle—this ability to generate and to radiate love that other people feel. It's one of the greatest secrets in life—that we always remain a source of love. Through the darkest, coldest times in our lives, we still have this capacity to renew our ability to love other people, to love nature, to love life and our highest ideals, and to love God. When we revive ourselves with love, our spiritual sunshine can light up the dreariest landscapes.

You will have disappointments, but never give up believing in love. Some day you will meet someone whose very existence will make you happy. Have the courage and faith to wait until the time comes when you have met the right person. Romantic love is not the only form or expression of love; but it can become a lifetime source of happiness.

WHAT IS LOVE?[129]

Love is joyful awareness. When we love we are being joyful about the existence of someone or something. We love when we let ourselves feel happy about anything that exists in the world. Love of life is being happy to be alive.

Think of babies and puppies, and how they make you feel. Think of a beautiful work of art or your favorite music. Think of anything that makes your heart sing, however faintly, and you will get at least an inkling of the importance of love in your life. Now imagine what it would be like if your whole life were about being a source of love.

Love makes us feel reverent and grateful. Love makes us treasure, nurture, and protect the person or the thing we love. It can be a family member or friend; it can be a dog or cat; it can be a garden. It can be a person, community, all of existence, or God. When we love, we want to take very good care of whomever or whatever we love.

THE FOUNDERS AND ROMANTIC LOVE

Very little has been written about the Founders and their attitudes toward romantic love or toward love in general; but I've been able to piece together some information about their feelings of attachment to other people, to the nation, and to God.

Romantic love requires a degree of equality between the sexes and this was sorely missing in many families in colonial America. The prevalent idea at that time was that "the man was not only the head of the family but that he was the family."[130] This inequality is not conducive to passionate, romantic love. People need to feel empowered in order to most fully express vulnerable feelings of love. But despite the station of women in early America, there are well-documented relationships of romantic love and devotion among the Founders. Also, people differ so much in their ideas about romantic love and about family life that it's no surprise that the Founders also varied in their attitudes and experiences.

John and Abigail Adams

John and Abigail Adams profoundly loved each other and, as a result, their marriage became enriched with the years. Both also cared deeply about their children who provided them with full measures of both joy and grief. One of their sons became a drunk who abandoned his family; another, John Quincy, became president of the United States.

John Adams, Advice to His Daughter Nabby on Choosing a Husband[131]

Daughter! Get you an honest man for a husband, and keep him honest. No matter whether he is rich, provided he be independent. Regard the honor and moral character of the man more than all other circumstances. Think of no other greatness but that of the soul, no other riches but those of the heart.

Among the Founders we have learned the most about, it is perhaps clearest that John Adams found lasting romantic love—what I'm calling real deep love—for a lifetime partner. When John and Abigail Adams were separated, they kept each other alive in their hearts and wrote as often as they could. When she was on her deathbed, a grief stricken John Adams wrote to his friend Thomas Jefferson:

> Now Sir, for my Griefs! The dear Partner of my life for fifty four Years as a Wife and for many Years more as a Lover, now lies in extremis, forbidden to speak or be spoken to.[132]

In his biography, *John Adams* (2001), historian David McCullough observed that John and Abigail were very much in love. McCullough believes that the marriage to Abigail was "the most important decision of John Adams's life." She would play such a dominant role in his life that, "for all his love for her," John Adams could not have anticipated her future importance to him. A profound love when handled responsibly produces unimaginably good results.

ABIGAIL ADAMS TO HER HUSBAND JOHN, APRIL 10, 1782[133]

Adieu my dear Friend. How gladly would I visit you and partake of your Labours and cares, soothe you to rest, and alleviate your anxiety were it given to me to visit you even by moon Light, as the fairies are fabled to do.

GEORGE AND MARTHA WASHINGTON

George Washington experienced his first love when he was a young man, but the relationship never was fulfilled. In a letter to Martha's granddaughter, he wrote skeptically and even negatively of passionate love, which he saw as inevitably losing its luster; but at the same time he called it a "necessary ingredient" along with the partner's good sense, reputation, disposition, and finances—all of which characterize his choice of Martha.

George Washington from a Letter to His Granddaughter[134]

Love is a mighty pretty thing, but, like all other delicious things it is cloying; and when the first transports of passion begin to subside, which it assuredly will do, and yield, oftentimes, too late, to more sober reflections, it serves to evince that love is too dainty a food to live on alone, and ought not to be considered further than as a necessary ingredient [in] that matrimonial happiness which results from a combination of causes: none of which are greater importance than the partner should have good sense, a good disposition, a good reputation, and financial means.

Washington may have married Martha in part for her status and wealth as a widow, as well as her many good qualities. Historians have doubted that they were romantically in love, but most of the evidence disappeared when Martha burned their letters shortly before her death. In one letter that survived, George wrote to her on June 23, 1775: "I retain an unalterable affection for you, which neither time or distance can change."[135]

In another of the few letters to his wife that have survived, Washington wrote to Martha from Philadelphia soon after hearing he was selected Commander-in-Chief of the Continental Army. Washington expressed a complex, touching mixture of love and concern for his wife, reluctance to sacrifice their mutual happiness, doubts about his own capacity as a general, faith in God, and a commitment to higher duty. In this book about the moral views of the Founders, it is enlightening to read a substantial excerpt from Washington's June 18, 1775 letter.

GEORGE WASHINGTON'S LETTER TO MARTHA, JUNE 18, 1775[136]

My Dearest,

I am now set down to write to you on a subject which fills me with inexpressible concern—and this concern is greatly aggravated and increased when I reflect on the uneasiness I know it will give you—It has been determined by Congress, that the whole Army raised for the defense of the American Cause shall be put under my care, and that it is necessary for me to proceed immediately to Boston to take upon me the Command of it. You may believe me my dear Patcy [nickname for Martha], when I assure you, in the most solemn manner, that, so far from seeking this appointment I have used every endeavor in my power to avoid it, not only from my unwillingness to part with you and the Family, but from a consciousness of its being a trust too far great for my Capacity and that I should enjoy more real happiness and felicity in one month with you, at home, than I have the most distant prospect of reaping abroad [away from Virginia], if my stay was to be Seven times Seven years. ... I shall rely therefore, confidently, on that Providence which has heretofore preserved, & been bountiful to me, not doubting but that I shall return safe to you in the fall—I shall feel no pain from the Toil, or the danger of the Campaign—My unhappiness will flow, from the uneasiness I know you will feel at being left alone—I therefore beg of you to summon your whole fortitude & Resolution, and pass your time as agreeably as possible—nothing will give me so much sincere satisfaction as to hear this, and to hear it from your own Pen.

Although she could easily have remained a woman of leisure in their mansion at Mount Vernon, Martha Washington spent every single winter with her husband George throughout the war from December 1775 through late 1783, including the desperate, freezing winter at Valley Forge. One of Washington's generals observed, "Mrs. Washington is excessively fond of the General and he of her. They are very happy in each other."[137]

Benjamin and Deborah Franklin

In dramatic contrast to John Adams and George Washington, Benjamin Franklin seemed emotionally distant from his wife, Deborah Read Franklin. Ben spent many years in London before the War of Independence, and then many years in Paris during the war. One historian found him very socially able but less competent at creating "deep personal commitments or emotional relationships, even within his own family."[138] Unlike Adams and Washington, his absences from home seem more like a preference than a necessary sacrifice.

Franklin was very well liked and fascinating to people; but he was not someone who easily made close attachments. His writing does not reflect a commitment to romantic love. We can contrast Washington and Adams who hated to leave home, Jefferson who adamantly resisted ever leaving home, and Franklin who seemed comfortable and happy away from home.

James and Dolley Madison

James Madison, who made so many contributions to the Constitution and the Bill of Rights, and who eventually became the fourth President of the United States, enjoyed a now famous marriage to Dolley Madison. James was greatly enamored with Dolley but he was notoriously shy. He asked Dolley's friend

Catherine Coles to write to Dolley on his behalf. Madison's stand-in explained in a letter to Dolley, "he thinks so much of you in the day that he has Lost his Tongue, at Night he Dreams of you…& he hopes that your Heart will be callous to every other swain [suitor] but himself…"

According to historian Richard Labunski, "although Madison seemed to be content with a life devoted to helping form the new nation, he became a happier and more fulfilled person after he married Dolley," and his letters to her "show a thoughtful and affectionate individual who was clearly enamored with his charming and outgoing partner."[139]

Benjamin and Julia Rush

Signer and physician Benjamin Rush had a strong romantic bent and deeply loved his wife Julia. When she had to be away with the children to seek safety from the pestilence in Philadelphia, Rush wrote poignantly to her about missing the opportunity to share the events taking place at the Second Continental Congress. He described his loneliness on returning each day to their empty home: "A melancholy silence reigns through every apartment of our house. Every room and piece of furniture proclaims that you are gone, and sympathizes with me in lamenting the absence of their mistress."[140]

In another letter he wrote, "My heart glows with an affection for you at this instant so tender, so delicate, and so refined that I want words to express it."[141] He spoke of being torn between his patriotism and his resentment at his duties to country taking him away from her.

Unlike Rush, most of the Founders did not readily express tender or romantic passion in their letters. They were reserved and valued their privacy. Remember that Martha Washington burned her correspondence with her husband before her death. In a state of extreme mourning after his wife's death, Thomas Jefferson also burned their complete correspondence.[142]

Franklin, Adams, and Washington were also aware that they were writing not only to the recipients of their letters but also for posterity, and this further inhibited them. There seems no doubt, however, that for Adams and Washington, as well as Jefferson and Madison, their wives were cherished partners. We have seen that Samuel Adams also was deeply attached to his wife and wrote her letters from the heart.

There can be no question that romantic love was alive and well in the colonies and in the hearts of many Founders, perhaps no less than we would find it in contemporary times.

The Founders Loved Life

The Founders were extraordinarily passionate about life. Adams, Washington, and Franklin as well as Rush and Madison, cared deeply about the lives of those around them—their friends, communities, and fellow citizens and even all of humanity and posterity. They risked their lives, their fortunes, and their reputations to fight for the independence of the colonies as well as their own personal freedom. Each one felt he was on a mission for all humankind. They wanted to contribute to freedom around the world now and forever. They cared enormously not only about the fate of America but also the fate of humankind.

Historians Michael and Jana Novak emphasize George Washington's loving connection to his soldiers. After describing how Washington trusted in a "benevolent Providence" during the dark times of war, they explain: "But there was another dimension to Washington's tie with his beloved army. He loved them." And they loved him back: "They loved even looking at him and gave him enthusiastic 'Huzzahs!' each time he appeared among them, usually on horseback." [143]

It is no exaggeration to say that Washington felt love for future generations who might benefit from the revolution for which he risked and sacrificed so much. In notes for his first inaugural address as president, Washington wrote that he would not live to see the grand effects of the American Revolution upon the world but that he "enjoyed" anticipating "the progress of human society and happiness" that would result. Washington elaborated:

> I rejoice in a belief that intellectual light will spring up in the dark corners of the earth; that freedom of enquiry will produce liberality of conduct; that mankind will reverse the absurd position that the many were made for the few; and that they will not continue as slaves in one part of the globe, when they can become freemen in another.[144]

Many of the Founders truly loved humanity and that love motivated their dedication to spreading liberty throughout the world.

Most of the Founders had numerous additional passions. Franklin brimmed over with curiosity and displayed intense interest in innumerable aspects of life covering technology, nature, science, philosophy, education, public health, medicine, community organizations, economics, politics, and society. A list of his interests and his actual contributions looks like a catalog of the major subjects being taught at a modern university.

Franklin was always busy improving the world around him, even taking on the painful issue of slavery in his last years. He immensely enjoyed the company of other people, and as already described, he was even criticized for how much fun he had socializing in Paris. While Franklin's manner was mellow and the depth of his emotions never fully shared, he was bursting full of life.

Adams loved his farm and home, and his family. He loved to read, he loved ideas about the law and politics, he wrote well, he enjoyed great oratorical skills, and he thrived on walking. He was a very serious man who could be seen as obsessed with duties and responsibilities, much like the young Ben Franklin who doggedly pursued his thirteen virtues. Adams was also extremely concerned about how history would remember him—and feared being lost in the giant shadows cast by Washington, Franklin, and Jefferson. But his anxieties should not obscure the more profound and loving motivations that guided his life.

Washington was devoted to life on his plantation. He was a great horseman and loved to ride and hunt. He was also a very serious man who shared with Adams and Franklin a profound conviction that the individual should perfect himself morally and improve his conduct in every possible way. That's one of their great gifts to us—the example of living by sound principles.

Adams and Jefferson Rekindle their Friendship

During their contest for the presidency following John Adams's first term in office, Adams and Jefferson fought bitterly with each other. After Adams lost to Jefferson, he and his wife Abigail had difficulty forgiving their old friend and colleague. But in their later years the two men reconciled, corresponded extensively with each other, and healed their wounds. Benjamin Rush played a role in their reconciliation, an example of how much the Founders often cared about each other.

As the 50th anniversary of the Fourth of July approached in 1826, both men were near death. Adams was ninety and Jefferson was eight-three, both too frail to last another year. Each knew he was at death's door and each wanted to survive until the 50th anniversary commemorating the signing of the Declaration of Independence. Each knew the other was dying and at least in Adams's case was aware of trying to reach the goal together. As if confirming that Providence still watched over them and their revolution, both men died on July 4, 1826—the half-century anniversary of the work they had accomplished together. The last or nearly last words on the lips of John Adams were "Thomas Jefferson lives."[145] Adams had no way of knowing that his friend would not live out the day.

THE FOUNDERS LOVED GOD

As we've seen, the leading Founders were not simply Deists—people who believe that God made the world like a watchmaker and then left it to go on ticking on its own. Washington, Franklin, Rush, and John and Samuel Adams each expressed the idea that only God's intervention in the War of Independence could account for America's victory over Great Britain. Washington attributed favorable outcomes in specific battles to Providence.

Another Founder can be added to the group, James Madison, who observed that the "finger of that Almighty Hand" had not only guided America to victory in the war, it had also wrested success out of the conflicted and tumultuous effort to write and to agree upon the U. S. Constitution.

JAMES MADISON, FEDERALIST PAPER NO. 37, 1787-1788[146]

The real wonder is, that so many difficulties [at the Constitutional Convention] should have been surmounted; and surmounted with an unanimity almost as unprecedented, as it must have been unexpected. It is impossible for any man of candour to reflect on this circumstance, without partaking of the astonishment. It is impossible, for the man of pious reflection, not to perceive in it a finger of that Almighty Hand, which has been so frequently and signally extended to our relief in the critical stages of the revolution.

John Adams, Washington, and Franklin did not speak of God or Jesus in the adoring and passionate way that was typical of many devout Christians at the time. During their lifetimes, America underwent a spirited Christian revival called the Great Awakening; but that was not the religious style of these three men. Their love for God was inseparable from duty and responsibility, and the determination to act bravely in accordance with His plan for humanity.[147] All three specifically welcomed God's hand in their lives, especially in regard to His intervention on behalf of the great Cause of independence.

Of the three, John Adams expressed the most joy in his awareness of God and of himself as a creature of God. In a letter to Jefferson, he wrote, "My Adoration of the Author of the Universe is too profound and too sincere. The Love of God and his Creation; delight, Joy, Tryumph, Exaltation in my own existence, tho' but an Atom, a molecule Organique, in the Universe, are my religion."

Jefferson studied and cited the teachings of Christ but at times challenged all religious dogma. We have seen that Jefferson feared God's justice toward those like himself who supported slavery. In *The Faiths of Our Fathers*, Alf J. Mapp, Jr. describes Jefferson's changing and contradictory religious views. Mapp quotes a letter written a little more than a year before Jefferson's death in which he advises, "Adore God...Love your neighbors as yourself, and your country more than yourself. Be just. Be true. Murmur not at the ways of Providence. So shall the life into which you have entered be the portal to one of eternal and ineffable bliss."

Adams, Franklin, and Washington deeply believed in "Do unto others what you would have others do unto you;" but they did so without expressing love for Jesus or for fellow Christians in the soaring, spiritual ways we find in the Gospels and among many colonists. For them, it seems, love and devotion to God were expressed through courage, good deeds, and responsible living. Often their references were to the God of the Old Testament who led the Jews from slavery to freedom.

By contrast, Benjamin Rush's life was infused with Christianity and his devotion to Jesus Christ as his savior. He wanted the Bible to be the centerpiece of public and private education. Like most of the Founders, Rush deeply believed in the actions of God in his own life. As a physician who has been called the Father of American Psychiatry, Rush already suffered from the unfortunate tendency of modern psychiatrists to view psychological and spiritual problems as biological in origin. Nonetheless, in concluding one of his essays on psychiatry, he makes clear that his last resort in time of stress was not "medicine" or psychiatry, but a belief in God:

> A belief in God's providence and a constant reliance upon his power and goodness, impart a composure and firmness to the mind which render it incapable of being moved by all the real, or imaginary evils of life.[148]

Love and Feeling the Presence of God

Most people I know who love each other feel the presence of God in their relationship. Their relationship feels sacred to them. Those who experience romantic love often feel that it is spiritual rather than physical in origin, and that it connects them to each other and also to something even greater than themselves.

A loving relationship is so wonderful it makes people feel blessed. My wife Ginger likes to say that we've won the love lottery. She's teasing, of course. She believes our relationship is a gift from Above.

The sense of God's presence is not only strong when we love each other; it can also be powerful when we love nature. Ginger and I live in a house on a lake facing the western sky. We can see the sunsets from almost any room in the house as well as from the front patio and gardens, and from the dock down the hill.

The lake stretches to our left and to our right as far as we can see, and so do the clouds that come down to us from the Great Lakes to the north.

When the sun sets, it floods the broad canvas, sometimes with a brilliant palette. The horizon becomes an ever-transforming stained glass window and the water shimmers with reflected colors. Most evenings, sharing the sunset, we feel as reverent as anyone could feel in church. We feel we are in church—His original church.

The appreciation of beauty is closely akin to love. The experience of beauty is the esthetic equivalent of love. When we feel that someone or something is beautiful, it brings us joy.

Why do feelings of love and an appreciation of beauty so often bring on a feeling of God's presence and often a profound gratitude to God? I believe that the desire to love and to experience beauty lies in that same core within us as our yearning to know God.

Almost all people who feel love also believe that their feelings of love have something divine about them. Especially when we are feeling very close to each other, we often feel close to God as well. And when people stop believing in love, they often stop believing in God as well. We love and appreciate beauty from the same spiritual source inside ourselves that we worship God.

Self-Love

Over the years as a psychiatrist, psychotherapist, and writer, I have puzzled mightily over the concept of self-love. When the Bible says, "Love your neighbor as you love yourself," it confirms that self-love is basic to human nature, admirable, and even the origin of love for others. But what does self-love mean? What does it feel like?

As I was finishing this book, some new thoughts came to me. Self-love may be our appreciation of the sacred core within us—our soul. That is why self-love is not "narcissistic," selfish, or self-centered. Our spiritual center doesn't belong exclusively to us. It is part of being human—the essence of human nature—implanted there, as the Founders would say, by nature and by God. It is the source of our capacity to appreciate freedom, to take responsibility, to feel gratitude, and to love. To love ourselves is to appreciate and to take joy in the gifts we have been given by nature and by God.

Love Banishes Conflict

Want to stop being self-centered? Love is the best answer. Want to find a way out of constant conflict with your family or friends? Love is the only genuine answer.

Love makes us feel joyful about the happiness of the person we love—making his or her interests as important to us as our own. Love can make the other person more important to us than ourselves, so that we become willing to sacrifice and even to risk death to protect our loved one, child, or friend. Love for any activity, from hobbies to careers, turns sacrifice into a "labor of love."

When we love, we no longer have self-interests; we have mutual interests. By making us at least as aware of the other's needs as our own, love banishes conflict. Love is to human life as clean air and water are to the environment; there cannot be too much of it, and everyone is nourished, everyone benefits.[149]

The Spiritual Glue of Life

As a psychiatrist, I have learned that it is impossible to be full of craziness and filled with genuine love at the same time. Love for anything, from another person to a set of ideals, will keep us sane. Unwillingness to love leads to withdrawal into an unreal, detached world. That's psychosis. We are "in touch with reality"—which means being in touch with other people—only to the degree that we love.

Love is the spiritual binding that holds our relationships together and that ultimately keeps us from falling apart. Starting with the love we receive in infancy from our mothers and other caretakers, love enables us to become fully human. We are made of each other physically and spiritually starting in the womb and then while nursing in infancy. We are put together with the spiritual glue called love.

Love Is a Perfect Guideline

When you experience love, you have a perfect guideline for how to behave—by appreciating, treasuring, caring about, protecting, and nurturing your loved one. When in conflict, the love guideline provides you a perfect solution—to put the other's interests on a par with our own and at times even higher. When two people do this—when both put as much focus on the desires of their loved one as they do on themselves—a marvelous relationship is born, a relationship that will not only empower the ones who love each other, but everyone they touch.

This is what makes a good friendship, partnership, or marriage succeed—each person is looking out for the other as much or more than for himself or herself.

When you love nature, the love guideline once again tells you to treasure, nurture, and protect your favorite patch of nature or even all of nature.

Love for their fellow human beings, for principles and ideals, and for God motivated leaders like John Adams, Samuel Adams, Washington, Rush and Franklin risk their lives, fortunes, and reputations. They cared more about the fulfillment of their principles and ideals, about their nation, about the future of humanity, and about God than about their own lives, fortunes, and reputations. This is also true of great modern leaders like Martin Luther King, Jr. and Mahatma Gandhi.

If You Love Humanity

If you love humanity—and understand the role of liberty, responsibility, gratitude, and love in human progress—you will create endless opportunity for yourself to gain strength and happiness by acting on behalf of the human race. As a loving person, you will be on firm ground whenever you try to help other people, provided that you never compromise their freedom, never discourage their personal responsibility and independence, and never diminish their desire to love and be loved.

When you love God, you can make Him a part of everything you do, increasing your happiness and your motivation to promote whatever aspect of His creation that you wish to bring joyfully within your awareness. Imagine putting God's interests above your own. Provided you do not get confused and imagine that you are God-like—provided that you remain humble in your understanding of God as a loving Creator who gave us individual freedom and responsibility—your devotion can transform your life for the better and spread strength and happiness far beyond yourself. This is one of the greatest lessons from our Founders.

Suffering from Loss of Love

Loved ones become so important that we suffer when we lose them. The loss can make us feel sad and, in the extreme, dismal, helpless and hopeless. The way to overcome this suffering is not easy but it is straightforward: Keep the lost love alive in your heart and never let your losses keep you from continuing to be a source of love.

During the War of Independence, the Founders had to maintain their love of liberty and their love of America through many years of fear and discouragement. John Adams was physically ill and alone in Europe. He continued with whatever energy he could muster to seek support from potential allies in France and Holland. George Washington, losing battle after battle, had to be satisfied with being able to retreat without losing his entire army. Both Adams and Washington were sustained by their love for their ideals and their country, as well as humankind and God, for whom they believed they were fighting. They also maintained their faith that God supported their cause. And as we saw, they were further sustained by the love they shared with their wives.

Never confuse suffering with love itself. Suffering is about the loss or absence of love. When love has been frustrated or lost, we disable ourselves if we decide to give up on ourselves as a source of love. Whether we are talking about romantic love or love for our nation, everything good and enjoyable has risk built into it—the risk of losing what we love. Fearfully trying not to get hurt is no way to live. It's not only worth daring to love—it's an absolute requirement for strength and happiness.

Always Remember, You are a Source of Love

Always remember that you are a source of love and that your ability to love can be an endless resource of strength and happiness for yourself and for everyone you inspire in your lifetime. Remember that each of us is like a spiritual sun—we can radiate our love to bring light, warmth, and energy to everyone and everything that surrounds us.

Remind yourself that in your deepest core you are a source of love—and you will quickly begin to refresh your strength and happiness. Take responsibility for being a source of love and you are guaranteed to make the most out of your life.

Try this. At a moment when you're feeling sad, hopeless, or depressed, remember who you are—a source of love. And then remember who and what you love. Even if you have lost someone you love and even if you have failed in an attempt to fulfill your dreams, you will rise above bitterness or depression as long as you keep alive within yourself the love you feel for your lost loved one or your dreams, and as long as you remain aware of being a continuous source of love.

To dare to love, we must risk losing who or what we love. The risk is not only worth it—it is essential to a fulfilling life. Whenever we give up being a source of love, we give up our strength and our happiness. We withdraw and become helpless and ineffective. But the moment we determine to once again become a loving person, we revitalize ourselves. We quickly know the direction we must take—to take joy in life and to act responsibly in nurturing and protecting those we love.

Want to know the ultimate secret of a strong and happy life? Be a source of love! Then handle love responsibly—working hard when necessary to treasure, nurture, and protect everyone and everything you love. Being free makes it easier to love but taking responsibility at all times and under all conditions is an absolute requirement for becoming a loving person.

Love is the fountain of strength and happiness. As long as you can find joy in any aspect of life, you will gain that much strength and happiness. As long as you experience beauty and as long as you love, you will keep your head above the emotional floodwaters and you will find ways to enjoy your life and to contribute to life even at times when you are struggling with what seems like endless gloom.

When you love your husband or wife, your mother or father, your child or friend—when they seem like beautiful treasures to you—you gain strength and happiness simply by reminding yourself that they exist. That's why we carry pictures of them in our wallets and on cell phones—because remembering our loved ones brings us strength and happiness. We gain even more strength and happiness when we take full responsibility for acting in a loving, protective, nurturing, and caring way toward those we love.

A person can be rich and yet miserable. A person can attain all of his or her most ambitious goals, and yet remain miserable. But it's impossible to experience yourself as a source of love without becoming happy.

In this chapter, unlike earlier ones, I have elaborated my own views beyond those of the individual Founders. I am not sure they would agree with all the nuances I have expressed about love; but I know that all of them, each in their own ways, deeply loved life and were committed to improving the lives of other human beings. They all believed in the Golden Rule.

If you want to have an extraordinary life—guaranteed—dare to feel and to express love at every opportunity. The more people and the more aspects of life in which you can find beauty and joy, the happier and more successful you will become. The more you love, the more you will increase your opportunities for happiness and success in life, and the more you will encourage those opportunities for others.

Chapter Thirteen

A Friend Who Lived By Basic American Values

The Founders thought a great deal about you and me—about building a nation that would continue to stand for freedom, human rights and individual responsibility. They wanted their ideals to live on as their gift to us.

As an American, you have as much or more opportunity to make something of yourself than anyone anywhere else in the world. Never give up on the basic American values of freedom and responsibility and never stop making them come true for yourself and your loved ones.

As a child or an adult, don't be afraid to make a difference. It is shocking to hear professors at our most prestigious universities arguing about whether or not the Founders were great men who really made a difference in history. Even some school teachers don't want children to believe in American heroes.

What a dismal place America will become if we stop believing in our great and heroic men and women. We need to believe that people can make a difference, even a huge difference, because the world will always present huge problems—and equally enormous opportunities. Children need to know that it's possible for individuals to make a significant difference when living with courage, determination and principles.

There was only one George Washington and one Martha, one John Adams and one Abigail. There was only one Ben Franklin. And there will be only one you or I as well. What we will do with the gift of our lives no one knows in advance—not even ourselves. Each life is full of surprises, some disappointing and some unexpectedly wonderful. This does not change as we grow older. Very little is certain about life except this—if we live by the values of liberty, responsibility, gratitude and love, we will make the most of whatever life gives to us. We will receive the most and we will give the most, and probably a lot more of both than we ever imagined possible.

The "Wow!" of all this is that you live in America, a nation founded on these principles—a nation in which you are free to take full responsibility for yourself and the fulfillment of your wishes and ideals. America is a place where children can grow up to become independent and where it's never too late for adults to learn the same lesson about the benefits of taking responsibility for oneself.

Meet George Peter

His name was George Peter. He died after a long, rich life, and the funeral was a day-long celebration that so inspired me that I came home and began the manuscript that eventually became this book.

Hundreds of people met on the broad front lawn of George's dusty old mansion on the shore of Cayuga Lake in the Finger Lakes Region of central New York State to share their stories about his life and how it had improved theirs.

The Finger Lakes are made from long, slender and deep crevices carved out by the glaciers as they slowly crept down from Canada thousands of years ago. Stamped like a giant open palm upon the terrain of upstate New York, the Native Americans referred to these lakes as God's handprint.

Fortunately, it was a beautiful day and under the blue sky people had much good to say about how George had touched their individual lives. Then a horse-drawn procession brought his body to the church on the campus of Wells College to which he'd also contributed his time. George loved parades and had organized many of them for his community but this was the first one in his honor. Dozens of members of the fellowship to which he belonged lined both sides of the church interior.

At the memorial, his neighbor and closest friend Steve spoke about how George had transformed his life by making him a better and more loving father and husband. As Steve later explained to me, George was more a model than an instructor. If you knew George and how he conducted himself, it made you want to be a better person. George became a kind of presence on Steve's shoulder reminding him of the right thing to do at the right moment.

The president of Wells College, a small liberal arts college located in George's hometown of Aurora, talked about how George had turned the village into a welcoming place so that every newcomer had the opportunity to feel at home. The next speaker was the past president of Cornell, the great university situated on top of a hill in Ithaca at the southern end of Cayuga Lake twenty miles to the south. This elderly, distinguished gentleman described how George had inspired people on every level from the workers on the campus to the president himself. In his straightforward, down-to-earth approach to people, George made no distinctions of rank among them. Even after George became one of the most influential men on Cornell's Board of Trustees, he never thought of himself as anyone more special than anyone else.

George not only became a human catalyst for creating a caring community wherever he went, he also eventually managed one of the most important projects in Cornell's history and in the history of science and engineering—the building and maintenance of the largest electronic telescope in the world.

George was also an amateur historian who especially loved and admired the Founders of our country. George and I understood and liked each other so quickly and thoroughly in part because we both believed in the four pillars of the good life—liberty, responsibility, gratitude, and love.

You may be thinking, "Wait! Wait! What lessons can I get from this man's life? I'm not some great man or woman who rubs elbows with the rich and famous. I'm not some mighty educator who helps to run universities. And I'm certainly not a physicist who can manage one of the great scientific projects of our time. I don't have that kind of background, education or charisma."

Well, neither did George Peter have that kind of background, education, or charisma. In appearance, George was unassuming. In stature, he was small, and his Armenian and Syrian heritage made him considerably darker in skin than the Brahmins of the Ivy League would have considered ideal. He grew up on a local farm under not particularly favorable emotional or economic circumstances. His family had neither wealth nor connections in the community.

George went to the local high school in Ithaca and when he was graduated, it was the only degree he would ever earn. This man who eventually managed an enormously complex and innovative scientific project didn't have a PhD—not even a college degree.

George joined the armed services in 1940 and married Gloria, the woman of his dreams, while stationed in the Midwest. He would love her into their old age together. When I met him several years after her death, he was still in mourning, and would remain so for the remainder of his life. When people talked of George, they often spoke of George and Gloria. She was with him all the time, giving him inspiration, love and comfort throughout his life. She was a person full of life who welcomed people into her home.

When George came back from World War II, he opened a small business repairing TVs in Ithaca. It didn't earn much, so he applied for a job at Cornell. This is what George wrote on that job application: "I have had nearly five years of electrical experience and am naturally mechanically inclined. Also I enjoy working with electricity more than any other type of work."[150]

George became the voice of the workingman on Cornell's illustrious academic campus. To empower the voice of the working staff, he founded a newspaper for them entitled *Pawprints*. It may have been the first of its kind—a university newspaper for the working staff—and it remains the largest. Eventually he was chosen to be the first non-academic member on the Board of Directors of an Ivy League university. Nor was he a token workers' representative; he became a leader on the board, including the search committee for selecting the president of the university.

The rest is the history of a life well-lived. Everyone George met, he strengthened and inspired in the most gentle, subtle fashion. I got to know George in the last five years of his life and, as you can readily see, he made an impression on me. When Steve's wife Randi told me at the funeral, "I'm glad you're here—George's newest best friend," it deeply touched me. As much as anyone I have known personally, George Peter lived by the principle of using his liberty in this great nation to take responsibility for living a productive and loving life.

Many things moved me deeply during the celebration of George's life but two stand out. One of his children explained that she had known a George Peter who was unlike the man that was being celebrated. Back then her dad had been a somewhat irritable man with a temper. He was not easy to be around or overflowing with love.

When she was ten years old, an older brother got into difficulty. Her parents were driving cross-country to rescue her brother from this circumstance and she was sitting alone in the backseat of the car. She remembers that her mom and dad were very quiet and sad. Then she heard her dad say something to her mother that she would never forget—that he must have done things terribly wrong for this to happen to one of his children. He concluded that he must become a better father.

From that day on, she said, she had a new father—the patient, even-tempered, caring and loving human being that everyone was celebrating more than sixty years later. She said it was the most important lesson of her life: That a person can decide to change for the better and then do it.

George Peter—as much as anyone I've ever known—found his essential gifts, took full responsibility for them, and shared them with as many people as he could. That's as good a goal as a person can have.

At the funeral, I was also impressed by something that George and I had talked about, our shared values. The memorial booklet for his celebration mentioned his belief in the nation's founding principles—of the right to life, liberty, and the pursuit of happiness. George and I had talked about how much we revered the Founders and what they had given to us. As a self-taught historian, George understood that human conduct on every level is governed by principles and that those principles are identical for the individual, the community and even the mightiest of governments. This was one of the gifts he received from the Founders of this country that guided his life to the end.

I don't want to leave you with the idea that George was perfect. For example, he could be quite stubborn. One colleague described how even in his late seventies this diminutive but hardy man insisted on swinging a sledgehammer to pound in the stakes of a tent at an outdoor university event. Especially because it was raining, his friend persuaded George to give up his hammer. With his usual congeniality, George readily agreed.

But a few minutes later George had found another sledgehammer and was once again swinging away.

George could get his ire up. A close friend told me about George's reaction to a much younger, larger man who had taken sidewalk politicking too far and was embarrassing a group of older women who disagreed with him about a community issue. This aggressive fellow, looking somewhat like an unkempt lumberjack, towered over George; but George intervened to tell him to back off from "the ladies." The larger man stuck a menacing finger into George's chest, George reacted with a flurry of defensive movements, and their brief scuffle had to be broken up. At the time, George was in his early eighties.

I met George a few years after his cherished wife Gloria had died. Although he never stopped missing her, he remained a charming and caring companion to everyone. He was eager to share ideas with me and to encourage me in new directions. He remained grateful for the life that had been given to him, and especially for his wife Gloria and her companionship. At the end, he seemed to have reached the point where he was ready to be with his wife. The story of his life was gliding slowly to a stop and he was prepared to begin another where he would be with Gloria again.

What the Life of George Peter Teaches Us

Like George Peter, all of us can take charge of our own personal lives and our family lives according to the principles of the Founders embodied in the Declaration of Independence and the Bill of Rights. We can take full responsibility for our own decisions and actions, and expect the same of our friends, family and everyone we deal with in our lives.

This may be the most important fact of life: You and I will do best and receive the most satisfaction when we take responsibility for our own lives and when we respect the right of everyone else we know to behave in the same way.

Personal freedom has limits. There will be times when you have to do things you do not want to do, for example, pass a test in order to get a driver's license, pay for a traffic ticket, and pay taxes on your income and your home. Government will be behind most of these limits on your freedom; and many of them are necessary, including obeying speed limits and paying some amount of taxes. Our sense of right and wrong will also place limits on our freedom.

But personal responsibility has no exceptions and no limits. You can decide to do what you know is right. You can decide for yourself to take complete responsibility for everything you do all the time. You can take responsibility for being honest, for being fair, and for opening your heart to friendship and love. You can be as charitable as you wish and take care of the needs of others to whatever degree you desire. You can decide for yourself about the balance between dependence and independence when you help friends or family, or give to charity.

You can find the courage and resolve to take complete responsibility for yourself, and the more fully you do, the happier and more productive you will be. Toward this goal, the following chapters look more closely at how to apply The Primary Principles to our personal lives.

Chapter Fourteen

The Four Primary Principles of a Good Life

Four familiar words capture the essence of the principles that the Founders applied to their daily lives and to their vision for the nation: freedom, responsibility, gratitude, and love.

Putting these four basic values into a single moral nutshell, we arrive at The Primary Principles:

The Primary Principles
Protect freedom.
Take responsibility at all times.
Express gratitude for every gift and opportunity.
Become a source of love.

All of the Founders we have met in this book conducted themselves by these principles. John and Abigail Adams, George and Martha Washington, and Benjamin and Deborah Read Franklin—each of them almost certainly would have endorsed The Primary Principles. Other Founders on whom we've spent less time—Samuel Adams, Benjamin Rush, Thomas Jefferson, and James Madison, as well as their wives whom we have only glimpsed—also seemed to try to live by the principles of freedom, responsibility, gratitude, and love.

The Founders worked hard, endured major deprivations, and risked everything to live by these principles. There are no shortcuts to self-esteem or to the good life. Living by good principles doesn't guarantee good fortune, an easy time, or even happiness. At times it can require extraordinary courage in both our personal lives and our public lives. But a principled life does guarantee that you will make the most of your abilities, control events and outcomes as well as possible, feel proud and satisfied with how you have conducted yourself, and give as much as possible to others and to the world. And with the help of good fortune and Providence, you will find happiness as well. So, ethical living doesn't guarantee a long and prosperous life, or happiness on this planet—but it does vastly increase the likelihood of achieving everything you want, including a good measure of success and happiness.

These four basic principles can help all of us to "live like Americans." Unless enough of us aspire to live by these ideals, we will lose our freedom and independence. The Declaration of Independence, U. S. Constitution, and Bill of Rights will no longer capture our hearts and minds, and we will succumb to a new tyranny.

The Four Hard and Fast Rules for a Successful Life

Drawing on The Primary Principles, here are four Hard and Fast Rules that guarantee the best possible life for you, your family and children, and everyone else you care about.

First, promote freedom by respecting the separateness and independence of everyone in your life, including every adult's right to life, liberty, property, and the pursuit of happiness. Make your own decisions as freely chosen as possible, consistent with your ethics and ideals. Teach children the principles of freedom and responsibility that they will exercise more fully as they become adults.

Second, implement responsibility by being aware of all your choices and decisions at all times—no exceptions. In taking responsibility, you affirm that you are always making choices and that it is up to you to make ones that are rational and loving, even under the most difficult and trying circumstances. Expect others to take responsibility, including children within the limits of their maturity.

Third, express gratitude by giving heartfelt thanks throughout each day for your life and the life around you. Expressing gratitude for all your gifts and opportunities will increase your satisfaction and appreciation of life and inspire you with a meaning greater than yourself.

Fourth, become a source of love—feel and express joy about every aspect of life. Protect, nurture, and treasure as many people and as much of life as you can. And accept love from others as well. Love will make you and those you touch feel more joyful about life and guide your actions in positive directions.

Almost all of the mistakes we make in life will involve deviations from living by The Primary Principles and the Hard and Fast Rules derived from them. From your family life to your work, re-examine any failure you have endured in your life to discover where you were lax in implementing freedom, responsibility, gratitude, or love. You will be able to locate your own contribution to the failure and to grasp how to avoid similar mistakes in judgment in the future.

Your Personal Moral Authority

In order to live by The Primary Principles and The Hard and Fast Rules, you must believe in yourself as a moral authority. You must believe that you have the right and the capacity to understand right and wrong, and to apply your understanding to life. You must believe that you are able to make choices and decisions based on sound values. If you have been shaken in this regard, and no longer believe in yourself as a moral authority, you will fail in your attempt to live by sound principles.

Nowadays we have been told to believe that everything is relative, that no one is right and no one is wrong, and that any one idea is as good as another. None of this is true, and in fact, it is impossible to live successfully from this viewpoint. When the Founders spoke about human rights being derived from nature and God, they meant that these rights are embedded within us and that we need to act upon them.

Remind yourself about this—that as much as George Washington, John and Abigail Adams, or Benjamin Franklin—or my friend George Peter whom you met in the previous chapter—you also have within you an essential spiritual core that generates eternal values, including freedom, responsibility, gratitude, and love. Remind yourself that you must, and I do mean must, live by these values in order to feel as good about yourself as possible and to have the best possible influence on the world around you.

Teaching Our Children

Even before they become able to walk and talk, children begin to develop their moral understanding during conflicts with their siblings and their parents. Infants see that their own actions draw reactions from the people around them. Without realizing it, and for better or worse, they begin to formulate rules for how to conduct themselves. Starting as early as possible in their lives, they need us to provide them moral authority.[151]

Toddlers express the freedom impulse in all of their activities. Set a two-year-old loose in an expansive garden or a toy store, and watch the child gleefully explore everything from flowers to toy trucks. The youngster's drive for unrestrained activity quickly comes into conflict with the convenience of adults, with safety, and with property rights. Children say "Mine!" about everything of interest and must learn to respect the property of others. They must be taught to recognize the difference between enjoying the smell of a flower and roughly pulling apart its petals.

Unfairness also becomes an issue very early in the toddler's life. Often it is connected to property rights as children fight over toys or grab for fragile objects that are treasured by adults.

The use of force also becomes a source of conflict and an opportunity for instruction. A frustrated fifteen-month-old, especially when feeling ill, can unexpectedly start biting or hitting.

It's up to us as parents, grandparents, older brothers and sisters, and teachers to instruct children about ethics and principles, encouraging their freedom while showing them the restraints required to live free in a republic. At the same time, we must provide them so much unconditional love that they will want to gain our approval and to learn from us. Our unconditional love will also nurture the feelings of confidence and self-worth that are necessary for the successful pursuit of life, liberty, property, and happiness.

A major purpose of this book is to provide information and principles for families to share together. Parents, grandparents and other caregivers of children must take responsilibity for being moral authorities in their lives.[152]

Courageously embrace that you are an American in the tradition of the Founders and that you can live by these American values. Believe in yourself as someone who can protect freedom, take responsibility, express gratitude, and act as a source of love. When you fully and enthusiastically embrace these values, you will become a moral authority. The men, women, and children in your life will recognize and benefit from the life-affirming strength that emanates from you, and you will become happier, more self-content, and more successful in fulfilling your dreams. You will be able to wake up and think, "Wow, I'm an American!"

Chapter Fifteen

Applying the Primary Principles to Our Lives

You are alive, and being alive, you have purposes. All living creatures have purposes, if only to stay alive. That's one way we can figure out that something is alive—we watch it trying to maintain its existence, to grow, and to reproduce itself.

Take a drop of water from a pond and put it under a microscope, and you will find a mob of tiny critters trying to stay alive. Step out into nature and sit quietly for a while. Under your feet and in the air, you will witness creatures trying to stay alive. Contemplate a city, and you will see the same thing—millions of people trying to stay alive.

But don't be fooled—human beings have much greater purposes and goals than merely staying alive. Think about yourself. No matter how young you are, or how old you are, you spend most of your time doing far more interesting things than trying to stay live. You are working, playing, exploring, learning, and sharing love—all day long.

Safety, security, and survival rarely become the first priorities of human beings. Even on the battlefield or during natural disasters, people almost always do more than try to stay alive. Usually they try to look out for each other and to take care of their children. If they are separated from their families, they think about them and may try to remain alive for their sake. If they are spiritual or religious, they often pray for their loved ones and try to be at one with God. If and when we Americans become oriented around safety, security, and survival, we will lose our energy, our zest, and our ability to determine the course of our own lives. We will lose our capacity to live courageously, even heroically in our own lives.

Remember how the Founders were willing to risk and even to sacrifice their families, fortunes, and lives fighting for their own freedom and the liberty of the colonies. Remember that not a single signer of the Declaration of Independence, nor a single wife of a signer, ever reneged, even under the greatest duress. They knew they were fighting not only for themselves but also for all humanity—the liberation of all human beings. They bravely devoted their lives to higher purposes—and so should we, if we want to have satisfying and fulfilling lives.

Physician and revolutionary Benjamin Rush was a keen observer of his fellow citizens during the War of Independence. Writing in 1788, he described how Americans believed that the future of the planet depended on their efforts:

> The controversy [the American Revolution] was conceived to be the most important of any that had ever engaged the attention of mankind. It was generally believed by the friends of the Revolution, that the very existence of freedom upon our globe, was involved in the issue [outcome] of the contest in favor of the United States.[153]

Hundreds of thousands of Revolutionary War soldiers and American colonists made their higher ideals far more important than life itself. Many thousands died. That's what Patrick Henry meant in his famous and impassioned speech, "Give me liberty or give me death!"[154] Human beings are not merely alive—they are motivated by higher purposes and ideals.

Patrick Henry to the Virginia Convention, March 23, 1775[155]

It is in vain, sir, to extenuate the matter. Gentlemen may cry, Peace, Peace — but there is no peace. The war is actually begun! The next gale that sweeps from the north will bring to our ears the clash of resounding arms! Our brethren are already in the field! Why stand we here idle? What is it that gentlemen wish? What would they have? Is life so dear, or peace so sweet, as to be purchased at the price of chains and slavery? Forbid it, Almighty God! I know not what course others may take; but as for me, give me liberty or give me death!

Applying Lofty Ideals to Your Down-to-Earth Life

Ideals aren't like fairytales or imaginary friends—they are real. They are a part of us and with us all the time. They can give us courage. If we choose our ideals wisely and keep them alive in our awareness, they can govern how we act and ensure that we make the most out of our lives.

If your life were suddenly put in danger—maybe you stepped in front of a truck or fell into a frigid pond—without thinking twice about it, your parents, husband, or wife would risk life and limb to save you. Firemen, police officers, and soldiers routinely put their existence in jeopardy because it's their job and they take responsibility for doing it right. People routinely do what's right rather than what might benefit them at the moment. So all living creatures have purpose and many human beings pursue very lofty purposes while carrying out their everyday lives.

Want to be the best possible son or daughter, husband or wife? The best possible friend or parent? The best possible worker, craftsman, artist, professional, or businessperson? The best possible citizen of your community, nation, and world? You will make the most of your life when you pursue your ideals with all your heart, mind, and soul. A good life is about taking responsibility for everything in our lives at all times in a manner that furthers our highest ideals, including the four pillars of the good life—freedom, responsibility, gratitude, and love. That's what I want to get across to you in this book. That's what our Founders, when at their best, wanted for themselves and for all of us.

The key to an extraordinary life—the heart of the Judeo-Christian and Enlightenment traditions, and the gift of the Founders—can be summed up in that simple but demanding guideline I call The Primary Principles:

THE PRIMARY PRINCIPLES
Protect freedom.
Take responsibility at all times.
Express gratitude for every gift and opportunity.
Become a source of love.

It requires courage and hard work to make freedom, responsibility, gratitude, and love your personal guidelines; but your choices will become easier and clearer—and you will be able to transform your life and the lives of everyone you touch. I agree with my friend and fellow psychiatrist William Glasser (1998) who makes choice the central fact of human psychology. He has applied these principles to therapy and to entire school systems. Psychologist Thomas Bratter has applied similar principles to the successful treatment of the most disturbed and undisciplined adolescents at the John Dewey Academy (2006). I have used these principles for decades as a psychiatrist treating the full range of human suffering and disorder. Living to the best of our ability requires taking responsibility for making choices based on rational principles and on love.

When you learn to consciously choose the direction of your life based on sound principles, you will be surprised to learn how many opportunities are available to you. Even in today's political climate you will be gratified to find how much personal freedom you still have. If you pursue the highest ideals, you will fill your heart with love for other people, for human creativity, for nature and the world around you, and for God.

Making the Most of a Marvelous Idea

Think about what a marvelous idea this is. You don't have to fuss about who you are, whether you're good or bad, or what kinds of goals and purposes you should pursue. Know that within you there is a spiritual center or soul that can create love and take responsibility for it—and then contribute to life. Then you can get to work making the most of who you are—protecting, nurturing, and educating your inner spirit so that it can flower and contribute to others.

Remember that when we love each other, we place great importance on each other's happiness. The act of loving makes us happy and it makes us want to see our loved ones happy as well. Even small children delight in making their parents happy. The vast majority of parents love their children so much that they routinely and gladly make sacrifices for their happiness. Always remember that no one loses and everyone gains when people love each other in a responsible fashion, including respect for each other's freedom and autonomy, and gratitude for each other's love. Striving to love others and to love life will bring you the greatest possible amount of joy and happiness.

Understanding the potential goodness that lies at your spiritual center will help in everything you decide, while of course you will have to figure out the details for yourself. What are you really best at doing? What do you really want to do? How can you make a living doing something you love? Will you find a soul mate or partner for life with whom you share deep love? How will you know when you find this person? How much balance should you give to advancing your own interests, the interests of your loved ones, and the good of other people? Can you make a life that includes all of these purposes at the same time?

You will have difficult and sometimes confusing choices to make but everything will become so much easier and clearer when you accept this one basic idea about yourself—that within you is a source of goodness that can be expressed through a loving and responsible life. You can keep coming back to that source within you when it's time to make decisions and to take new directions. You can ask, "Is my new choice or direction consistent with what I know about myself—that I am free to make my own choices, that I am able to love, and that I will prosper when I take responsibility for living in a way that protects, nurtures and supports other people and all of life?" Evaluate your actions by the standards expressed in The Primary Principles—freedom, responsibility, gratitude, and love—and you will enjoy life and give more to others than you ever imagined possible.

We may live in good times or bad ones. Human history at times makes progress, often in fits and starts, and sometimes it takes tragic deviations and violent regressions. There is no guarantee of continued human progress. Our own progress as individuals depends on Providence combined with our willingness to stand up for freedom, to take responsibility, to express gratitude, and to love. But regardless of the ups and downs of life, when we live by our highest ideals, we guarantee making the most of whatever is given to us in our own lives. We also guarantee contributing as much as we can to human progress in everything we do.

Human Nature and Human Flaws

When the Founders looked at human nature and at the actions of human beings, they saw flaws. The wisest of them like Washington, Adams, Franklin, and Madison knew that no one was perfect and that none of us could become anything close to perfect. They had no faith that people would always do the right thing, and so they focused on protecting individuals from being oppressed by each other and by their government; and they believed that education, both religious and secular, was critical to bringing out the best in citizens. In their minds, no government could make up for a poorly educated, badly informed, and misguided public.

After reflecting on our human nature, the Founders drew conclusions about liberty, responsibility, and democracy. They saw a mixture of human desires or aspirations—some rational and some irrational, some self-centered and some altruistic. Most important to them and to us, they saw that we could make choices and pursue what was good, for example, the attitudes ennobled in the Golden Rule. The choice was up to us as individuals, and they wanted to give us as much choice as possible.

The Founders also saw that human beings need freedom in order to make choices and to express their nature most completely and with the greatest satisfaction. From that, they concluded that freedom was a natural right. After all, why would we have been given the abilities to make choices and to take responsibility, if we were not intended to exercise them?

The Founders knew that we must work hard to take responsibility for our self-development; but they were mainly focused on what we can and should do for other people. Remember Ben

Franklin's life? He served others with wonderful inventions like the lightning rod and the Franklin stove, by supporting the War of Independence, by helping to create important ideas and documents like the Declaration of Independence and the U. S. Constitution, and by developing great schools and institutions. After reaching an age when most men are retired or even deceased, he took up the dangerous and difficult cause of opposing the institution of slavery.

Ben Franklin tapped into that source inside each of us that is good and that has love at the center of it. When we love each other, nature, or God—we express that spiritual center or essence. I believe that personal responsibility lies within our core as well. When we decide to always do what's right—we are drawing from that same spiritual source. When we take full responsibility for loving, nurturing, and preserving all of life—we are at our best.

The Founders did not believe that the capacity to live democratically was built into our human nature or that it came easily to us. But they thought that some form of self-government was the best approach to protecting individual human rights and self-expression. Some degree of democracy, like government itself, was a necessary evil or the best alternative among difficult choices. They constructed so many checks and balances to make sure democracy would not degenerate into mob rule or to one interest group dominating another. Individual rights, and not democracy, were their first priority.

Democracy was modified into what is called a republic—a democracy with restraints to limit the power of the many over the few and to reduce the risk of deteriorating into tyranny. The bedrock of a good society begins with freeing individuals to optimize their own lives without trampling on the equal rights of others. It's worth remembering how George Washington put it after the creation of the United States of America—from now on there would be no excuses; it would be up to us as individuals to make the best of our lives.

Confronting the Inevitable Unfairness of Life

There's not much about life that's easy or fair. In many parts of the world children are dying of disease, starvation, and abuse. People continue to slaughter and to oppress each other, sometimes by the millions. Even in America, there are many grave inequalities and injustices. Sometimes taking public stands at grave risk to myself, I have devoted much of my own life to reform work on behalf of children and others who have been abused by my profession of psychiatry.[156]

Yes, life can be daunting; but the answer is not to give up on the principles of freedom, responsibility, gratitude, and love. If you wish to contribute to reforming and improving society, you can do it best by promoting and implementing the Founding principles of this great nation wherever and whenever possible.

The current economic downturn and loss of confidence among Americans has been caused, more than anything else, by the abandonment of the principles of freedom and responsibility that originally made this country great. Worse yet, our country has been put on a course that runs roughshod over these principles and instead exalts charismatic leadership and big government.

We are facing critical choices now and in the coming years. A new political tsunami is flooding the nation from sea to shining sea, and washing away the principles of the Founders. Individual freedom is no longer a topic of serious discussion. Personal responsibility is seen as a mirage. Hardly anyone promotes independence.

The new politics panders to the worst in human nature—fear and helplessness. It tramples on the inspired values of the Founders who built a nation that would protect the freedom of individuals to pursue their own life, liberty, property, and happiness.

Confronting Our Personal Fears

In today's economic climate, many people have lost their jobs and can't pay their bills. Others have lost their life savings or found themselves unable to help their children as much as they would like to. Yes, times are tough and it's easy to become discouraged and embittered. But we should never allow these feelings of helplessness to drive us into giving up freedom and personal responsibility.

The Founders taught us how to handle the good times and the bad—with respect for liberty, with uncompromising personal responsibility, with profound gratitude, with love for others, and with appreciation of a Meaning greater than ourselves. Live this way and you are guaranteed the best possible life under any and all circumstances. With luck or the blessing of Providence, you will create what feels like a miraculous life.

America remains a wonderful place to live—a country whose principles are worth fighting for and where individuals have considerable opportunity to choose the direction of their lives. We can still awaken every morning giving thanks that we live in the land of liberty and responsibility. We can throw our feet over the edge of our bed and celebrate the opportunity to live like an American. Then we can get out of bed and begin another day of bravely taking responsibility for living and enjoying our lives—and for doing our best to put the nation back on a course that's guided by its founding principles.

The Greatest Challenge of All

As difficult as life seems at times, the greatest challenge usually lies inside us. It's the challenge of making the most of our own unruly human nature. The colonists won their freedom from an oppressive king, but the far greater challenge was learning to manage their own domestic affairs according to their very high ideals for human rights. They responded by creating the first great nation based on liberty and individual responsibility.

At stressful and disheartening times, we need to reaffirm our own personal independence and our determination to live by our highest ideals. The most threatening reality is the tumult inside our own heads. The most dangerous mob is the one made up of our own riotous emotions. That's why many people suffer the most emotional stress under relatively good circumstances. We sometimes need a challenge or threat to distract us from our inner turmoil and to focus us on acting more responsibly and courageously in the external world. When we master ourselves and become moral authorities over our own lives, we become heroes in our own lives.

The stresses that the world puts on us are usually nothing compared to the stresses we put on ourselves. The hardest challenge of all is to develop, maintain, and expand our own moral authority over ourselves at all times regardless of circumstances. If we keep this in mind—that the key to success and happiness begins with our own attitudes—then we can maximize our chance for success and happiness under any and all conditions.

Instead of resenting our circumstances, we can feel and express gratitude for every opportunity and indeed for every breath we take that allows us to be alive as responsible and loving human beings. We can choose to live freely, responsibly, and with love—with the ultimate goal of making the world a better place.

When we act responsibly we feel good about ourselves. We feel self-esteem. Beyond self-esteem, love is the fountain of happiness. The final step in maturity and happiness is to become a source of love.

INTEGRITY AND LOVE

The Founders believed in the inherent integrity or wholeness of our human nature, something I envision and describe as a single, integrated inner source of everything good about us. The Founders concluded that the attributes of our human nature led us to possess certain inalienable human rights, "among them life, liberty and the pursuit of happiness." The leading Founders concluded that God had implanted this basic nature within us and that it made no sense to corrupt or to waste it.

The Founders also believed that the individual's life should be integrated around a coherent and cohesive set of values. They saw private and political values as inextricably linked and believed that the new republic could survive only as long as a morally enlightened citizenry supported it. Samuel Adams, the journalist and political organizer—a man who was deeply religious as well as politically radical—found a direct correspondence between how people live their personal and their public lives. Adams wrote, "no People will tamely surrender their Liberties, nor can any be easily subdued, when Knowledge is diffused and Virtue is preserved. On the contrary, when People are universally ignorant and debauched in their Manners, they will sink under their own Weight without the Aid of foreign invaders."[157] According to Samuel Adams, those who wish to destroy the liberty of a people will "practice every Art to poison their Morals."[158]

Samuel Adams on the Correspondence Between Private and Political Virtues[159]

He who is void of virtuous Attachments in private Life, is, or very soon will be void of all Regard for his Country. There is seldom an Instance of a Man guilty of betraying his Country who had not before lost the Feeling of moral Obligations to his private Connections.

By "virtuous attachments" Samuel Adams was talking about ethical human relationships. I believe that love forms our deepest attachments and connections, and also inspires our strongest values and ideals. Love cements friendship and family relationships, and inspires patriotism and devotion to humanity. Our impulse to love springs from that same spiritual center from which responsibility, duty, and obligation flow. Our devotion to life, liberty, responsibility, and the good of others—one and all, these spiritual impulses emanate from our sacred core. Ultimately, it's the origin of the yearning to know God. Make yourself familiar with yourself as a spiritual being with all these wonderful attributes. This spiritual source within each of us can light up our lives and the lives of those around us.

See yourself as a source of love, take responsibility for guiding your love in the right direction, and you cannot stray too far from living a good life. Love is the energy of life and responsibility is the determination to guide it properly. If you conduct yourself in this manner, how could your life—or anyone else's—go astray?

What Is Your Last Resort?

Our last resort is the place, person, idea or value we turn to when our backs are to the wall, when we seem to have no other alternatives, when all seems lost, or when we especially need a boost to live life in a principled, courageous, loving, and hopeful manner. Some people turn to their last resort only when they are facing extreme stresses but others turn to it on a daily basis. Our last resort in life defines us as individuals and guides our choices and actions.

Many Americans today are very confused about their last resort. As I've described in several of my previous books, many turn to psychiatrists and psychiatric drugs as their last resort, either on a daily basis throughout their lives or during emotional crises. Others turn to alcohol and illegal drugs. As a psychiatrist, I have found that people cannot build successful lives by relying on drugs that impact on the brain and mind. To build successful lives, people must learn to live by sound principles and higher ideals.

Chapter 12 examined the role of love in our lives and defined love as joyful awareness of any aspect of life including other people, nature, beauty, higher ideals, and God. Love encourages us to protect, nurture, treasure and revere whatever or whomever we love. Anything or anyone we love can become our source of moral sustenance and inspiration. For many, their last resorts are friends and family, or work. Many others turn to religion, spirituality, and God. And of course individuals rely upon different last resorts at different times and under different circumstances.

My wife Ginger pointed out to me that the Founders were "last resort people who lived in last resort times." In many ways this is true. The Declaration of Independence was a last resort document that the signers put their names upon only after heavy deliberations and many attempts at reconciliation with Great Britain. They knew that they and many others might pay with their lives for their independence. They turned to war only when all other alternatives were exhausted.

Although with less urgency and less potential calamity hanging over their heads, the Founders created the Constitution only after the failure of the less centralized government under the Articles of Confederation. They felt it was their last resort for the creation of a strong and enduring nation.

We have also seen that the Founders relied heavily upon living by their principles and ideals, and that the Founding Mothers and Fathers often had close and loving relationships with each other.

But one aspect of the Founders' lives clearly stands apart as their Last Resort—Providence or God. Remember how the signers concluded their Declaration of Independence in 1776:

> And for the support of this Declaration, with a firm reliance on the protection of Divine Providence, we mutually pledge to each other our Lives, our Fortunes, and our sacred Honor.

Remember Washington's acknowledgement of Divine Providence stated in his First Inaugural Address as President of the United States in 1789:

> No people can be bound to acknowledge and adore the Invisible Hand which conducts the affairs of men more than those of the United States. Every step by which they have advanced to the character of an independent nation seems to have been distinguished by some token of providential agency.

If I have been surprised by one thing in particular in my research for this book, it is the uniformity with which the Founders believed that God guided both their personal lives and the nation's struggle for independence. We have seen this reliance on Providence or God in the lives of Founders like John and Abigail Adams, George Washington, Benjamin Franklin, Benjamin Rush, James Madison, and Samuel Adams. Even Thomas Jefferson at times expressed fear of God's judgement and hope for His ultimate forgiveness and approval.

Knowing that there are solid truths about human nature and knowing the function of higher ideals in our lives can help to sustain us. Recognizing that these truths have been given to us by a Higher Power can do much more than sustain us—it can inspire us toward a fuller, more satisfying, and more effective life.

Can you work hard, succeed, and find happiness without being grateful for everything you receive? Maybe, but I doubt it. Being grateful, especially to God, is woven into our spiritual core along with all the other threads that make up the spiritual ball of yearning that is our soul. Without gratitude we tend to sink into its opposite—resentment, bitterness, and even despair.

Can we be loving and responsible without believing in God? Yes, we can; but without faith in Someone or Something greater than ourselves, it's easy to fall short of our full potential, especially our capacity to experience joy and to share happiness. By going it alone, and relying only on ourselves and other fragile human beings, we make it unnecessarily hard on ourselves and on others. Most Americans, much like the Founders of our nation, find great strength in a loving God who cares about us and who intervenes on occasion in our affairs here on Earth.

Not Perfect, But Working Hard at It

Sometimes we have to struggle with our darker impulses and sometimes we must face conflicts with other people to stay on course. Bringing out the best in our human nature requires persistent hard work. We must aim at taking responsibility all the time under all circumstances, while remaining a source of love. Founders like George Washington, John and Abigail Adams, Benjamin Franklin, Samuel Adams, and Benjamin Rush devoted their lives to consciously developing and perfecting their integrity. In a surprising consensus, they agreed that the ultimate service to God consists of doing good deeds for others.

The Founders knew there were limits to perfecting themselves, but they tried never to shirk the task. It was a lifelong effort for them. This may be their greatest lesson and legacy—that we can work hard to guide our lives by basic truths that spring from within our very nature. They taught us to live in accordance with our love for liberty and our devotion to personal responsibility, independence, other human beings, and God.

This is no exaggeration—The Founders cared about future generations, sometimes more than for themselves; they cared that much about you and me. They risked everything, and some sacrificed everything, to offer us the freedom to exercise responsibility in the pursuit of our own happiness and the happiness of everyone we touch throughout our lives. They were not merely fighting for their own personal advantage during their lifetimes; they were fighting for universal rights for everyone on Earth in future times.

What the Founders taught us about living can be summed up in The Primary Principles:

The Primary Principles
Protect freedom.
Take responsibility at all times.
Express gratitude for every gift and opportunity.
Become a source of love.

When we live by these principles we promote American values at their best and we help to preserve the American dream for everyone, including future generations of people throughout the world. At the same time we maximize our opportunity to live a good life in which we contribute as much as possible to our loved ones, our community, and our nation. This is the vision that the Founders gave to us—principles to build a nation upon, principles to build a life upon. It's a vision that can inspire our lives and the lives of people everywhere in the world.

Bibliography

Allen, W. B. (2008, April 3). Rising By Falling: George Washington: The Concept of Limited Presidency. From Historians on America. Retrieved on December 30, 2008 from www.america.gov/publications/books/historiansonamerica.html

Appleby, Joyce. (2003). *Thomas Jefferson*. New York: Time Books

Bailyn, Bernard. (1992). *The Ideological Origins of the American Revolution, Enlarged Edition*. Cambridge, MA: The Belknap Press of Harvard University Press.

Bennett, William J. (2006). *America: The Last Best Hope. Volume I. From the Age of Discovery to a World at War, 1492-1914*. Nashville, Tennessee. Nelson Current.

Bratter, T. E., Bratter, C. J., Coiner, N. L., Kaufman, D.S. & Steiner, K. M. (2006). Motivating gifted, defiant, and un-convinced students to succeed at The John Dewey Academy. *Ethical Human Psychology and Psychiatry, 8*, 7-16.

Breggin, Peter. (1992). *Beyond Conflict: From Self-Help and Psychotherapy to Peacemaking*. New York: St. Martin's Press.

Breggin, Peter. (1997). *The Heart of Being Helpful: Empathy and the Creating of a Healing Presence*. New York: Springer Publishing Company.

Breggin, Peter. (2002). *The Ritalin Fact Book: What Your Doctor Won't Tell You about ADHD and Stimulant Drugs*. Cambridge, Massachusetts: Perseus Books.

Breggin, Peter. (2009). "Live Like an American!" Regular radio reports on the nationally syndicated talk show Savage Nation. Audio and transcripts available on www.breggin.com

Brodsky, Alyn. (2004). *Benjamin Rush: Patriot and Physician*. New York: St. Martin's Press.

Brookhiser, Richard. (1997). *America's First Dynasty: The Adamses, 1735-1918*. New York: Free Press.

Compston, Christine, and Seidman, Rachel Filene (Eds.). (2003). *Our Documents: 100 Milestone Documents from the National Archives.* New York: Oxford University Press.

D'Souza, Dinesh. (2008, November). Created Equal: How Christianity Shaped the West. *Imprimis, 37* (11), 1-5.

Ellis, Joseph. (1996). *American Sphinx: The Character of Thomas Jefferson.* New York: Vintage Books.

Ellis, Joseph. (2002). *Founding Brothers: The Revolutionary Generation.* New York: Vintage Books.

Ellis, Joseph. (2007). *American Creation: Triumphs and Tragedies at the Founding of the Republic.* New York: Vintage Books.

Fehrenbach, T. R. (1999). *Greatness to Spare: The Heroic Sacrifices of the Men Who Signed the Declaration of Independence.* Bridgewater, New Jersey: Replica Books.

Ferling, John. (2002). *Setting the World Ablaze: Washington, Adams, Jefferson, and the American Revolution.* New York: Oxford University Press.

Ferling, John. (2007). *Almost a Miracle: The American Victory in the War of Independence.* New York: Oxford University Press.

Fischer, David Hackett (2004). *Washington's Crossing.* New York: Oxford University Press.

Fleming, Thomas. (2006). *George Washington's Secret War: The Hidden History of Valley Forge.* New York: Smithsonian Books.

Glasser, William. (1998). *Choice Theory: A New Psychology of Personal Freedom.* New York: HarperCollins.

Goodman, John C. (2009). A Prescription for American Health Care. *Imprimis,* 38 (3), 1-5.

Green, Harry Clinton, and Green, Mary Wolcott. [1912]. *The Pioneer Mothers of America.* New York: G. P. Putnam's Sons. Excerpted and republished as *Wives of the Signers.* (1997). Aledo, Texas, WallBuilder Press.

Griffith, II, Samuel (2002). *The War for American Independence: From 1760 to the Surrender at Yorktown in 1881.* Chicago, Illinois: University of Illinois Press.

Hamilton, Alexander, Madison, James, and Jay, John [1787-1788] (2006). (Robert A. Ferguson, Ed.) *The Federalist*. New York: Barnes & Noble Classic.

Henriques, Peter. (2006). *Realistic Visionary: A Portrait of George Washington*. Charlottesville, VA: University of Virginia Press.

International Center for the Study of Psychiatry and Psychology

(ICSPP). (Eds.) (2009) *The Conscience of Psychiatry: The Reform Work of Peter R. Breggin, M.D.* Ithaca, New York: Lake Edge Press.

Isaacson, Walter. (2003). *Benjamin Franklin: An American Life*. (2003). New York: Simon & Schuster.

Kaminski, John P. (Editor) (2008). *The Founders on the Founders: Word Portraits from the American Revolutionary Era*. Charlottesville, Virginia: University of Virginia Press.

Ketcham, Ralph (Ed.) (2003). *The Anti-Federalist Papers and the Constitutional Convention Debates*. New York: Signet Classic.

Labunski, Richard. (2006). *James Madison and the Struggle for the Bill of Rights*. New York: Oxford University Press.

Langguth, A. J. (1988). *Patriots: The Men Who Started the American Revolution*. New York: Touchstone.

Locke, John. (1682). *An Essay on Human Understanding*. London, England: Thomas Tegg.

Lossing, B. J. [1848] (1995). *Signers of the Declaration of Independence*. Aledo, Texas: Wallbuilder Press.

Mac, Toby, and Tait, Michael. (2004). *Under God*. Minneapolis, Minnesota: Bethany House.

Mapp, Jr., Alf. (2003). *The Faiths of Our Fathers: What America's Founders Really Believed*. New York: Bowman & Littlefield.

Mayer, Henry. (1991). *A Son of Thunder: Patrick Henry and the American Republic*. Charlottesville, Virginia: University Press of Virginia.

McCullough, David. (2005). *1776*. New York: Simon & Schuster.

McCullough, David. (2001). *John Adams*. New York: Simon & Schuster.

McDougall, Walter. (2004). *Freedom Just Around the Corner: A New American History, 1585-1828.* New York: Perennial.

Middlekauff, Robert. (2005). *The Glorious Cause: The American Revolution, 1763-1789.* New York: Oxford University Press.

Novak, Michael, and Novak, Jana. (2006). *Washington's God: Religion, Liberty and the Father of Our Country.* New York: Basic Books.

Philbrick, Nathaniel. (2006). *Mayflower: A Story of Courage, Community, and War.* New York: Viking.

Runes, Dagobert. (Editor) (undated). *The Selected Writings of Benjamin Rush.* New York: Philosophical Library.

Rush, Benjamin. (1970). *The Autobiography of Benjamin Rush.* Westport, Connecticut: Greenwood Press.

Smith, Adam. [1776]. (1982). *The Wealth of Nations.* New York: Penguin Books.

Stoll, Ira. (2008). *Samuel Adams: A Life.* New York: Free Press.

Strauss, Barry. (2004). *The Battle of Salamis. The Naval Encounter that Saves Greece—and Western Civilization.* New York: Simon & Schuster.

Wood, Gordon. (2004). *The Americanization of Benjamin Franklin.* New York: Penguin Press.

Notes

Archaic spelling within quotations has occasionally been corrected.

1 *The Works of John Adams, Vol. 4*, (Novanglus, Thoughts on Government, Defense of the Constitution). NO. III, paragraph 118. Retrieved January 11, 2009 from http://oll.libertyfund.org/index
2 Kaminski, 2008, p. 10
3 Ellis, 2002, pp. 133-134
4 Ferling, 2002, p. 123
5 Novak and Novak, 2006, p. 115
6 Langguth, 1988, p. 150. Sons of Liberty was a revolutionary Boston society led by Samuel Adams
7 Stoll, 2008, pp. 48-49
8 Levin, 2009, p. 126
9 Fehrenbach, 1999, p. 15. Ferling, 2007, p. 29
10 Ferling, 2000, p. 97. Estimates vary. Griffith, 2002, p. 168, estimates fewer British and more American casualties
11 Griffith, 2002, p. 168
12 From Ralph Waldo Emerson's *Concord Hymn* (1837)
13 Brodsky, 2004, p. 109
14 Brookhiser, 2002, p. 26
15 Strauss, 2004, p. 13
16 Strauss, 2004, p. 13. Translation by Strauss
17 McCullough, 2005, p. 55
18 Ferling, 2007, p. 56
19 Griffith, 2002, p. 186 for the casualty counts
20 Griffith, 2002, p. 186
21 Middlekauff, 2005, p. 322
22 Brookhiser, 2002, p. 26
23 Brookhiser, 2002, p. 25
24 Brookhiser, 2002, p. 26
25 Ferling, 2002, p. 164
26 Compston and Seidman, 2003, provide an accurate resource for documents described in this book, as well as brief descriptions of their creation
27 McCullough, 2005, p. 71
28 Stoll, 2008, p. 171
29 Stoll, 2008, pp. 171-2. Spelling in original
30 Stoll, 2008, p. 171
31 Fehrenbach, 1999, p. 247
32 Lossing, 1995, fn. pp. 91-92
33 Fehrenbach, 1999, pp. 246-247
34 Isaacson, 2003, p. 224
35 Griffith, 2002, p. 533
36 Green and Green. 1912, fn p. 280
37 Green and Green, 1912, pp. 278-279

38 Green and Green, 1912, from the unnumbered Contents page. Also see descriptions of Signer's and their families hardship in Fehrenbach (1999)
39 Stoll, 2008, p. 174
40 Stoll, 2008, p. 7
41 Stoll, 2008, p. 89
42 Stoll, 2008, p. 66
43 McCullough, 2005, pp. 106-107
44 Isaacson, 2003, pp. 315-316
45 Exodus 20; Deuteronomy 5. Also see Leviticus 19
46 Summary by Peter Breggin, borrowing from various sources
47 Other versions of the Ten Commandments combine 1 and 2, and make an additional Ninth Commandment specifically not to covet thy neighbor's wife
48 In the original, we are commanded not to covet our neighbor's wife, servants or slaves
49 Leviticus 19:18
50 Mark 12:30-31
51 McCullough, 2001, p. 453
52 Rush, 1970
53 Stoll, 2008, p. 8
54 Locke, 1682, p. 40
55 Isaacson, 2003, p. 261
56 Labunski, 2006, p. 102; Ellis, 2000, p. 61
57 Ferling, 2002, p. 16
58 Griffith, 2002, p. 263, fn
59 Runes (undated), p. 325
60 Fischer, 2004, p. 24
61 Appleby, 2003, p. 138
62 Ellis, 1996, p. 102
63 Bailyn, 1992, p. 139. See www.samueljohnson.com for quotes from Dr. Johnson.
64 Rush, 1970
65 Bennett, 2006, p. 90
66 Bennett, 2006, p. 105
67 Bennett, 2006, p. 103
68 Ketcham, 2003, p. 288. The quote is from the anti-Federalist essay by "Brutus" dated January 24, 1788
69 Bennett, 2006, pp. 103-104
70 The 17th Annual International Military and Civilian Combat Stress Conference, Marina del Rey, California, April 30-May 3, 2009, sponsored by Psycho-Legal Associates, Inc. and organized by Dr. Bart Billings. Dr. Breggin gave a full-day workshop on "Clinical Psychopharmacology" and spoke on "Does Psychiatric Medication Increase the Risk and Prevalence of Suicide?"
71 Retrieved on May 24, 2009 from http://www.army.mil/aps/09/2009_army_posture_statement_web.pdf
72 Ellis, 2007, p. 35
73 Ellis, 2007, p. 35
74 Ellis, 2007, p. 35
75 Fischer, 2004, p. 8, for reproduction of painting
76 Fischer, 2004, p. 435 for commentary and 436 for reproduction of painting

77 French engraving retrieved on December 8, 2008 from http://en.wikipedia.org/wiki/william_Lee_(valet)
78 Fischer, 2004, p. 18
79 Fischer, 2004, p. 25
80 Reproduction of painting retrieved on November 24, 2008 from www.mountvernon.org/index.dfm/fuseaction/print/pid/133/sti/3/sis/21
81 Ferling, 2002, p. 277
82 Henriques, 2006, p. 9
83 Henriques, 2006, p. 7
84 Henriques, 2006, p. 10
85 Mac and Tait, 2004, p. 13
86 Henriques, 2006, p. 22
87 McCullough, 2005, p. 113
88 For more about Samuel Shaw's service with the Continental army, see *Pennsylvania Magazine of History and Biography* published by The Historical Society of Pennsylvania, 1877, July, p. 281. Digitized by Goggle. Retrieved December 24, 2008 from http://google.com/books
89 Kaminski, 2008, p. 474, a letter from Samuel Shaw to Francis Shaw
90 Ferling, 2007, p. 185
91 McCullough, 2005, p. 191
92 Fleming, 2006, p. 317
93 Labunski, 2006, pp. 20-21.
94 Novak and Novak, 2006, p. 187
95 Fleming, 2006, p. 190.
96 Fleming, 2006, p. 189
97 Fleming, 2006, pp. 347-348
98 McCullough, 2001, p. 70
99 Wood, 2004, p. 9
100 Isaacson, 2003, p. 213
101 Wood, 2004, p. 228
102 Ellis, 1996, p. 88
103 Kaminski, 2008, pp. 146-148, quotes from Adams's letters, diary and autobiography
104 Kaminski, 2008, p. 150, Franklin letter of March 12, 1781 to the President of Congress
105 Isaacson, 2003, p. 468
106 Isaacson, 2003, p. 467
107 Isaacson, 2003, p. 4
108 See chapter 13
109 Labunski, 2006, p. 12
110 Hamilton, Madison, and Jay, 2006, p. 9
111 Mapp, 2003, p. 39
112 McDougall, 2004, p. 304
113 Lossing, 2007, p. iv
114 Ketcham, 2003, p. 47
115 D'Souza, 2008, p. 5
116 Stoll, 2008, p. 98
117 Mayer, 1991, p. 30
118 Mapp, 2003, p. 118

119 Ellis, 1996, pp. 65-66
120 Ellis, 2007, p. 33
121 McCullough, 2001, p. 225
122 McCullough, 2001, p. 224
123 Second Epistle of Paul to the Thessalonians, 3:2; cited in Mac and Tait, 2004, p. 93
124 Mac and Tait, 2004, p. 93
125 Philbrick, 2006, p. 165
126 Novak and Novak, 2006, p. 88
127 McCullough, 2001, p. 415
128 Goodman, 2009, pp. 2-3
129 Breggin, 1992
130 Appleby, 2003, p. 13
Green and Green, 1912, p. 9
131 McCullough, 2001, p. 289
132 Kaminski, 2008, p. 17
133 Kaminski, 2008, p. 5
134 Henriques, 2006, p. 103
135 Retrieved on December 12, 2008 from http://gwpapers.virginia.edu/documents/revolution/martha.html
136 Spelling corrected or updated. Retrieved on December 12, 2008 from http://gwpapers.virginia.edu/documents/revolution/martha.html.
137 Retrieved on December 12, 2008 from www.mountvernon.org/learn/meet_george/index.efm/pid/364
138 Isaacson, 2003, p. 44
139 Labunski, 2006, p. 260
140 Brodsky, 2004, p. 104
141 Brodsky, 2004, p. 105
142 Appleby, 2003, p. 13
143 Novak and Novak, 2006, p. 83
144 Allen, 2008, p. 3
145 McCullough, 2001, p. 646
146 Hamilton, Madison, and Jay, 2006, p. 200
147 Novak and Novak, 2006, Chapter 12, discuss Washington's religious attitudes
148 Runes (undated), p. 226. The essay is "On the Different Species of Phobia"
149 Breggin, 1992 and 1997, more extensively discuss the role of love in conflict resolution, and other issues touched on in this chapter
150 The job application letter and also the subsequent story about the sledgehammer are taken from a tribute to George Peter from *Pawprint*, August 15, 2008, the newspaper he founded for the "Cornell Community." www.pawprint.cornell.edu
151 Breggin, 2002, describes parental moral authority and its application to childrearing.
152 Breggin, 2002, criticizes medication treatment of children and describes better alternatives, including improving the role of parental moral authority
153 Runes (undated), p. 325
154 Mayer, 1991, p. 244 ff describes Henry's dramatic delivery and its effects
155 The speech was recreated from the memory of observers. Retrieved on December 12, 2008 from http://www.ushistory.org/documents/libertydeath.htm

156 See Peter Breggin's many books about psychiatric reform and about children. Also see International Center for the Study of Psychiatry and Psychology (Eds), 2009, for a book documenting the impact of Breggin's reform work

157 Stoll, 2008, p. 172

158 Stoll, 2008, p. 96

159 Stoll, 2008, p. 172

Acknowledgments

I want to thank several busy people and families for reading this manuscript, offering encouragement, and making suggestions. Chris and Elizabeth Harper, and their daughter Celia, made many useful comments and timely encouragement. Chris is a professor of journalism at Temple University where he teaches the history of American journalism, so his support was especially inspiring and his feedback very useful. Barry Strauss is a professor of history at Cornell and an excellent writer, and once again his support and comments were very valuable.

Psychiatrists Douglas Smith (Alaska) and William Glasser (Los Angeles), and educator Brian Kean (Australia), took the time to read the manuscript and to communicate their enthusiasm for it.

My friends Susan Close and Nadine De Santo devoted considerable time and energy to reading the manuscript. From grammatical details to thematic issues, their observations made this a better book. Yet another friend, Jay Ardai, applied his keen intelligence to reading the manuscript. I am very fortunate to have all of you for friends.

Ginger's mom Jean as always lent her loving encouragement.

Ginger remains inseparable from everything worthwhile that I do. As she has done with so many of my books, Ginger provided the most thorough editorial guidance. She was my constant intellectual companion throughout the writing process. I have published more than twenty books with some of the best publishers in the world, but for a variety of reasons we made a decision to self-publish *Wow, I'm an American!* Especially, we were eager to get the book out quickly at this critical time in

American history. From the cover photo and design to the selection of type, Ginger designed the physical book and directed its publication. She has received training and guidance from our friend Douglas Holleley, who teaches book design and publishes lovely books of photography. His inspiration and influence made this a better book.

About the Author

Peter R. Breggin, M.D. is a psychiatrist in private practice in Ithaca, New York, where he treats individuals, couples, and families with children. He is a strong advocate for psychological, social, and educational services that encourage independence, responsibility, and love.

Dr. Breggin is the world's leading critic of simplistic biological psychiatry and a lifelong proponent of more principled and caring approaches to helping people in distress. Many of his cutting edge criticisms of conventional drug-oriented psychiatry have now become widely accepted and have been affirmed by the FDA and the courts.

Dr. Breggin's radio report titled "Live Like an American!" regularly plays on the national talk show Savage Nation where he presents his unique combination of psychological and political commentary. It is heard on 250 stations. Dr. Breggin's radio reports can be listened to and the transcripts retrieved from his website: www.breggin.com. In addition, he writes a blog on Huffingtonpost.com that can also be found on his website.

A new book, *The Conscience of Psychiatry: The Reform Work of Peter R. Breggin, MD* (2009), brings together more than seventy original contributions describing the impact of Dr. Breggin's work on the fields of mental health and education. Sponsored and edited by the International Center for the Study of Psychiatry and Psychology (ICSPP), *the Conscience of Psychiatry* also draws on media reports spanning more than fifty years and other historical sources.

Dr. Breggin is a graduate of Harvard College and the Case Western Reserve School of Medicine. He has taught at numerous universities including the George Mason University Institute for Conflict Analysis and Resolution, the Johns Hopkins

University Department of Counseling, and most recently as a Visiting Scholar at SUNY Oswego's Department of Education in New York, the region where he and his wife Ginger now live. He is also a former Teaching Fellow at Harvard Medical School and a former fulltime consultant at the National Institute of Mental Health (NIMH).

Dr. Breggin is the Founder and Director Emeritus of the International Center for the Study of Psychiatry and Psychology (www.icspp.org) and Co-Founder with his wife of the scientific journal, *Ethical Human Psychology and Psychiatry.* ICSPP and its journal are the leading voices for reform in the field of psychology, psychiatry, and mental health.

He is the author of dozens of scientific articles and more than twenty books. His most recent popular book is *Medication Madness: The Role of Psychiatric Drugs in Cases of Violence, Suicide, and Crime* (2008, now in paperback). His most recent medical book is *Brain-Disabling Treatments in Psychiatry: Drugs, Electroshock and the Psychopharmaceutical Complex* (2008). Some of his earlier books include *Toxic Psychiatry* (1991), *The Heart of Being Helpful* (1997), *Talking Back to Prozac* (with Ginger Breggin, 1994), *The War Against Children of Color* (1998, with Ginger Breggin), and *Reclaiming Our Children* (2000).

Dr. Breggin's views have been covered innumerable times in all major print media and nearly all major radio and television sources. Print media include *Time, Newsweek, New York Times, Washington Post, Washington Times, Los Angeles Times, People, Psychology Today,* and *Human Events.* He has been heard or seen on radio and television shows across the political spectrum, including Oprah and Larry King Live many times, 20/20, 60 Minutes, Nightline, Hannity and Colmes, Hannity's America, Rush Limbaugh, The O'Reilly Factor, Lars Larson, and Laura Ingraham.

For additional information, please visit www.breggin.com.

LaVergne, TN USA
20 April 2010
179895LV00004B/179/P